WHO IS LIKE UNTO THEE?

O Lord among gods

David J Parker

Grosvenor House
Publishing Limited

The right of David J Parker to be identified as the author of this
work has been asserted in accordance with Section 78
of the Copyright, Designs and Patents Act 1988

The book cover is copyright to David J Parker

This book is published by
Grosvenor House Publishing Ltd
Link House
140 The Broadway, Tolworth, Surrey, KT6 7HT.
www.grosvenorhousepublishing.co.uk

A CIP record for this book
is available from the British Library

ISBN 978-1-80381-442-1

For Bridget
They also serve

TABLE OF CONTENTS

PREFACE

This book has been developing, like an embryo in the womb, for seven years. The first part which was originally called 'Can You Make It Up the Mountain?' was a study of the nature and character of our God so far as He has chosen to disclose it to us through the scriptures. The second part is probably summed up as 'How we should react to what we learned from the ascent of the mountain.' Perhaps subtitled 'The Challenges of Discipleship.' It is inspired by the writings of a 15th century monk, and I suspect, will be a greater challenge than the trek up the mountain.

So, this is an account of one man's journey following Christ; out of his love for God and his desire for obedience, he was compelled to undertake this quest with little understanding or just how much he would have to rely on the one he was so desperately seeking. He has likened his journey to that of a mountaineer, and similar to such an adventurer, he learned some hard lessons, had moments of rest and moments of pushing on with great determination. He now invites you to share in his experiences and embark on your own journey up the mountain and into the dark night. Do not think however, that you will be able to make it by relying on your own strength and wisdom; that will come from God. However lonely the climb might be, rest assured that you will never be travelling alone; as promised, the comforter, the Holy Spirit, will be there to guide, encourage, sustain, and motivate you.

Please treat this labour of love like a banquet; a feast of exquisite delicacies, each individual dish to be savoured and absorbed before indulging in the next.

PART 1

CAN YOU MAKE IT UP THE MOUNTAIN?

CHAPTER 1

MUSINGS FROM BASE CAMP - REGARDING HIS STEADFASTNESS AND HIS RELIABILITY

Father has 'invited' me to go up the mountain. Even after so many years of walking with the Lord there is still a sense of mild trepidation coupled with excitement and anticipation. Like Moses I have to go alone, no one is to share the journey with me, and images of the mountain present a very formidable picture; a journey not to be undertaken lightly and certainly not one to be undertaken in the strength of the flesh but only with the conviction and guidance of the Holy Spirit.

Before starting the climb, I have to give some retrospective consideration of who it is that I am expecting to encounter at the top, that is- if I make it that far! God is not some geriatric benefactor in a white nighty; someone who is only there to hand out gifts and monotonously reiterate "there, there everything will be alright, it can only get better". This sort of image and those that reinforce it by distorting the Word are an anathema to Him.

Let us first establish one vital truth:- *He does not change*! "God is not human, that he should lie, not a human being, that he should change his mind. Does he speak and then not act? Does he promise and not fulfil?"[1] From the psalms:- "Your word, Lord, is eternal it stands firm in the heavens."[2] "But the plans of the Lord stand firm forever, the purposes of his heart through all generations."[3] "In the beginning you laid the foundations of the earth, and the heavens are the work of your hands."[4] Then the prophets; "I the Lord do not change. So you, the descendants of Jacob, are not destroyed!"[5] "The Lord Almighty has sworn, "Surely, as I have planned, so it will be, and as I have purposed, so it will happen."[6] "The grass withers and the flowers fall, but the word of our God endures forever."[7] "I make known the end from the beginning, from ancient times, what is still to come. I say, 'My purpose will stand, and I will do all that I please"[9] And from the newer testament; "Jesus Christ is the same yesterday and today and forever."[9]

"Because God wanted to make the unchanging nature of his purpose very clear to the heirs of what was promised, he confirmed it with an oath."[10] "Every good and perfect gift is from above, coming down from the Father of the heavenly lights, who does not change like shifting shadows."[11] And from the Acts of the Apostles "They did what your power and will had decided beforehand should happen."[12]

I am Berean by rebirth (Cf: Acts 17:11) "Now the Berean Jews were of more noble character than those in Thessalonica, for they received the message with great eagerness and examined the Scriptures every day to see if what Paul said was true." In view of all the inadequate teaching being propagated today I am surprised that this is not standard practice among believers. Remember the Bereans only had the older testament, the Tanakh, to refer to; let me emphasise that we need to take on board the *whole* of Scripture and check out all teachings on this basis, perhaps this is what Jeshua meant in Matthew 13:52 "He said to them, "Therefore every teacher of the law who has become a disciple in the kingdom of heaven is like the owner of a house who brings out of his storeroom new treasures as well as old." We must not be swayed by those who disseminate stuff based on part truth, distorted truth, bias, downright lies and even blasphemy and heresy, all of which goes on in the so-called Christian church. And remember too that these guys were checking out Paul, the same one who penned a large proportion of our newer testament!

Bearing in mind this principle, it is prudent to consider one of our human hangovers from Adam and Eve's lust for knowledge and wisdom; the need to understand. This is especially prevalent in western(ised) cultures- the Greco-Romano mindset. The need to analyse, dissect, scrutinise, evaluate, and investigate everything, the insatiable lust for head-knowledge. The Hebrew mindset is different, it is God-centred, their IQ is not their god. They treasure the wisdom that comes from the God of Abraham, Isaac, and Jacob. If one is to go up the mountain, one has to adopt the Hebrew mindset and abandon the seductive nature of the spirit that 'needs to know'. Praise God I am in this place; at one time of my life, even after I was born again, I used to think that head knowledge was an end in itself, I enrolled with the Open University to study maths but one of the first level courses I went on was the basic science course which included a week of summer school at Reading University. I came out of it with a hunger for all sorts of knowledge. I got into chemistry, geology, physics and even history (no biology- it's too gory!). Like some of the academics we tend to listen to today, my intellect was my god; I thought the sun shone through my IQ! Now I know better; a couple of Proverbs are appropriate here:- "Trust in the Lord with all your heart and lean not on your own understanding;"[13] "Those who trust in themselves are fools, but those who walk in wisdom are kept safe."[14] If I was translating this verse I would call them 'idiots'; how can any intelligent person be so stupid as not to perceive the futility of worshipping his own knowledge, and ignoring God's? For it is written: "I will destroy the wisdom of the wise; the intelligence of the intelligent I will frustrate."[15]

Here 'wisdom' has been introduced, Wikipedia defines it thus:- Wisdom is the ability to think and act using knowledge, experience, understanding, common sense, and insight. I would say that it the acquired skill to know what you have to do with your knowledge. This, I think, is more of what God would expect when the Holy Spirit imparts that gift to us; "To one there is given through the Spirit a message of wisdom, to another a message of knowledge by means of the same Spirit,"[16] One gem of wisdom which I (by the grace of God) have acquired is that no-one is ever going to understand God. He has made it abundantly clear to me that it is pointless to try and understand Him and His ways, He has told me that He will give me knowledge on a 'need to know' basis; to ask why? is futile. If I need to know He will tell me, otherwise I am to mind my own business unless it is His business too!

Just to provide the evidence for this truth I apply the Berean principle again:- "The secret things belong to the Lord our God, but the things revealed belong to us and to our children forever, that we may follow all the words of this law."[17] Job expressed this wonderful truth most perfectly several times "And he (God) said to the human race, "The fear of the Lord; that is wisdom, and to shun evil is understanding."[18] "Can you fathom the mysteries of God? Can you probe the limits of the Almighty?"[19] "Do you listen in on God's council? Do you have a monopoly on wisdom?"[20] "The Almighty is beyond our reach and exalted in power; in his justice and great righteousness, he does not oppress."[21] From the Proverbs of Solomon, son of David, King of Israel; "Do not be wise in your own eyes; fear the Lord and shun evil."[22] "The fear of the Lord is the beginning of wisdom, and knowledge of the Holy One is understanding."[23] He expressed this sentiment again in two of his psalms "Before a word is on my tongue you, Lord, know it completely. You hem me in behind and before, and you lay your hand upon me. Such knowledge is too wonderful for me, too lofty for me to attain."[24] "Great is the Lord and most worthy of praise; his greatness no one can fathom."[25]

The writer of the book called 'Ecclesiastes' has always been a controversial figure, but he too acknowledged these eternal facts; "He has made everything beautiful in it's time. He has also set eternity in the human heart; yet no one can fathom what God has done from beginning to end."[26] "Then I saw all that God has done. No one can comprehend what goes on under the sun. Despite all their efforts to search it out, no one can discover its meaning. Even if the wise claim they know, they cannot really comprehend it."[27] "All this also comes from the Lord Almighty, whose plan is wonderful, whose wisdom is magnificent."[28]

Said the great prophet Isaiah, "Who can fathom the Spirit of the Lord, or instruct the Lord as his counsellor?"[29] "Do you not know? Have you not heard? The Lord is the everlasting God, the Creator of the ends of the earth. He will not grow tired or weary, and his understanding no one can fathom."[30] "Remember the former things, those of long ago; I am God, and there is no other; I am God, and there is none like me."[31] The New Testament continues to make the same proclamations; "My goal is that they may be encouraged in heart and united in love, so that they may have the full riches of complete understanding, in order that they may know the mystery of God, namely Christ, in whom are hidden all the treasures of wisdom and knowledge"[32] "Where is the wise person? Where is the teacher of the law? Where is the philosopher of this age? Has not God made foolish the wisdom of the world?"[33] "For the foolishness of God is wiser than human wisdom, and the weakness of God is stronger than human strength."[34] These are the things God has revealed to us by his Spirit. The Spirit searches all things, even the deep things of God."[35] "The mind governed by the flesh is hostile to God; it does not submit to God's law, nor can it do so."[36] "Oh, the depth of the riches of the wisdom and knowledge of God! How unsearchable his judgements, and his paths beyond tracing out! Who has known the mind of the Lord? Or who has been his counselor?"[37]

More musings to follow on the gift of God's wisdom and perhaps other topics I guess- as the Holy Spirit leads. Stay tooned for a report from the foothills, the lower slopes of the mountain where one might take a breather before the going gets steeper and rockier!

CHAPTER 2

A PERSPECTIVE FROM THE LOWER SLOPES - REGARDING HIS WISDOM AND HIS INFALLIBILITY

Not too demanding so far, a slight rise towards the foothills, but the meadow is still green with an abundance of streams and pleasant vegetation. The foothills can be clearly seen however, and are, without doubt, significantly steeper. In the distance the mountain proper looms into view with its steep slopes strewn with rocks and boulders; chasms and fissures are in view, and no obvious well-used passages to suggest a way up which has already been well-trodden by earlier pilgrims. Having established, hopefully, that my anticipated encounter involves a God who is absolutely unchanging, steadfast in His intent, immutable and sacrosanct; enigmatic, inscrutable, and unfathomable; one has further aspects of His character to consider and take account of. It is established that His wisdom is beyond our capacity to comprehend but He has granted a portion to us through the ministry of the Holy Spirit, this is how and why Paul can say "Who has known the mind of the Lord so as to instruct him? But we have the mind of Christ."[1] This is not for a few super-spiritual believers, but it is the normal Christian life! If you have truly died to yourself and become a disciple as defined by Jeshua Himself:- "In the same way, those of you who do not give up everything you have cannot be my disciples." (The *only* definition of a disciple in the whole of Scripture); then you can expect to have the mind of Christ and remember- He was a first century

Jewish Rabbi with a Hebraic mindset. This is not heresy, I repeat "we have the mind of Christ" 20 or so translations all say the same!

So, the wisdom of man is idiotic so far as God is concerned. Whoa! Don't bother telling me to appreciate what man with his 'wisdom' and intellect has done! "Just look at the advances in science and technology, the amazing medicines and machines we have invented, the exploration of the globe and now of space, the understanding of the body and mind etcetera," some will say. "Really? Then, if we are so wise and clever, why are there still thousands and thousands dying daily of thirst, hunger and disease?; why are such a lot of our 'sophisticated' implements and machinery designed specifically for killing people?; why are there so many people with broken minds and emotional issues, addictions, depressions and desperations?; why are we still, even in this country, the United Kingdom, still buying and selling each other?; why are we throwing thousands of tons of good food away every year?; why are we still exploiting each other when some have so much they don't know what to do with what they have?; why are doctors abandoning their own people to go after the big buck?" Are you one of those 'super idiots' who proclaim there is no God then turn round and say, "why does He allow all this stuff to happen?" The answer, my friends is not 'blowing in the wind' it is that He is asking *you* exactly the same question! If your reply is "what is the use I can't make any difference" then perhaps you would care to accompany me up the mountain, you might discover something to make you change your mind. So, if you still think you are a bit of a smarty-pants let me help discover the only source of real wisdom. "For to one is given the word of wisdom through the Spirit, and to another the word of knowledge according to the same Spirit."[3] Way back in Deuteronomy this truth is revealed:- "Now Joshua son of Nun was filled with the spirit of wisdom because Moses had laid his hands on him."[4] In Exodus we are informed that God told the Israelites "Tell all the skilled workers to whom I have given wisdom in such matters that they are to make garments for Aaron, for his consecration, so he may serve me as priest."[5]

Have you caught on to the only source of true wisdom? It is from God alone through the Holy Spirit! Where did Solomon acquire his gift? Answer:- "So God said to him, "Since you have asked for this and not for long life or wealth for yourself, nor have asked for the death of your enemies but for discernment in administering justice, I will do what you have asked. I will give you a wise and discerning heart, so that there will never have been anyone like you, nor will there ever be."[6] "God gave Solomon wisdom and very great insight, and a breadth of understanding as measureless as the sand on the seashore."[7] Then there was Job, a man blameless and upright who feared God and shunned evil,[8] who thought; "Age should speak; advanced years should teach wisdom. But it is the spirit in a person, the breath of the Almighty that gives them understanding."[9] In Acts we read "Brothers and sisters, choose seven men from among you who are known to be full of the Spirit and wisdom. We will turn this responsibility over to them."[10]

No! They are *not* independent gifts; as we have seen, having the Spirit is prerequisite to having the wisdom. Want to debate the matter? More evidence is available:- "Opposition arose, however, from members of the Synagogue of the Freedmen (as it was called), Jews of Cyrene and Alexandria as well as the provinces of Cilicia and Asia who began to argue with Stephen. But they could not stand up against the wisdom the Spirit gave him as he spoke."[11] "My message and my preaching were not with wise and persuasive words, but with a demonstration of the Spirit's power, so that your faith might not rest on human wisdom, but on God's power."[12] "It is because of him that you are in Christ Jesus, who has become for us wisdom from God- that is, our righteousness, holiness and redemption."[13] "What we have received is not the spirit of the world, but the Spirit who is from God, so that we may understand what God has freely given us."[14] "For this reason, since the day we heard about you, we have not stopped praying for you. We continually ask God to fill you with the knowledge of his will through all the wisdom and understanding that the Spirit gives."[15] "My goal is that they may be encouraged in heart and united in love, so that they may have the full riches of complete understanding, in order that they may know the mystery of God, namely Christ, *in whom are hidden all the treasures of wisdom and knowledge.*"[16] "I keep asking that the God of our Lord Jesus Christ, the glorious Father, may give you the Spirit of wisdom and revelation, so that you may know him better."[17] Final words on the subject (for now anyway) from James and John. "But the wisdom that comes from heaven is first of all pure; then peace-loving, considerate, submissive, full of mercy and good fruit, impartial and sincere"[18] "But when he, the Spirit of truth, comes, he will guide you into all the truth. He will not speak on his own; he will speak only what he hears, and he will tell you what is yet to come."[19]

Having debated the question of wisdom it has led me to ponder the 'wisdom' of continuing the trek up the mountain. Am I wise enough to have an understanding of where I might be going? (Rhetorical question!). Is ignorance bliss? - the trouble is I am not ignorant. I have been walking with the Lord a long time and have learned much at considerable cost. One thing I have learned of utmost importance through the ministry of the great prophet and judge, Samuel, who poses the question and then provides the answer:- "Does the Lord delight in burnt offerings and sacrifices as much as in obeying the Lord? To obey is better than sacrifice, and to heed is better than the fat of rams."[20] "Walk in obedience to all that the Lord your God has commanded you, so that you may live and prosper and prolong your days in the land that you will possess."[21] I might ponder on this in greater depth further up the mountain. In the meantime, though, I know that when Father 'invites' you to do something it is a smart move to do it! So, I guess that it is the gift of wisdom that I have been blessed with which persuades me to prepare myself as best I can, which means spending time being still and knowing that He is God, and waiting on Him to renew my strength. "Be still and know that I am God; I will be exalted among the nations, I will be exalted in the earth."[22] "Even youths grow tired and weary, and young men stumble and fall; but those who hope in the Lord will renew their strength. They will soar on wings like eagles; they will run and not grow weary; they will walk and not be faint."[23]

Now I am being refreshed and will be eager to press on; I know the next phase will be steeper and rockier, the first obstacles will probably be encountered and maybe the first of any trying to follow me up the mountain will be discouraged or even inclined (pun intended) to abandon the climb. I shall probably discuss some other characteristics of the Holy One who inhabits the peak.

CHAPTER 3

THE INITIAL CLIMB - HIS WILL AND FREE WILL

The slope is fairly steep now, the way is not well defined and there are probably three or four options with regard to which route to take. We shall take a look first at some of the characteristics of the One True God which are by and largely avoided. While musing, still on the issue of wisdom, how wise is it to persistently endorse the cases that are being presented with the Scriptures? Are they infallible? How can we know? Can we be sure that we are operating under that wisdom which comes from the Holy Spirit? Does God actually talk to us, if so, how do we know it is Him? Just consider for a moment; if God could not, would not or just did not talk to us He would be no God at all- would He?

Better sit and rest awhile, I think, more than enough here to keep one occupied during the start of the more difficult stages of the climb. First, before addressing some of the other questions, it might be wiser to establish another fact, another spiritual truth, one of those not mentioned much. God is utterly selfish! Oh dear, have we encountered an obstacle? Is the white whiskered, white suited 'Father Christmas' image being tarnished? You bet! God said to Moses, "I am who I am! This is what you are to say to the Israelites: 'I am' has sent me to you."[1] "God saw all that He had made, and it was very good."[2] Really? You believe that God created the whole lot? Yes! Mankind has decreed that he has figured out how it all started, the big bang. First there was absolutely nothing and then, in a minute fraction of a nano-second, the universe appeared. Wow! They are so smart; they are going to figure out now what actually happened in the big bang and tell us all about it. But haven't we heard this story before? Isn't the big bang another summary of the act of creation? If something doesn't exist at one instant in time but does exist in the next, then it has to have been created, doesn't it? Why are the 'intelligentsia' telling us the same story that has been told and read for thousands of years and strut about as if they have just made the discovery of all time. Fact is that the discovery of all time was made in the garden of Eden when Adam and Eve discovered that God was utterly selfish! We shall discuss this topic in greater detail later in the discourse when we investigate His attitude towards love.

We need to assess the fallibility or otherwise of the Scriptures, but we will come back to that; it might involve retracing some of our steps and going a slightly different route, but we shall see. In the meantime, I shall insist that they and the Holy Spirit are the only legitimate and infallible source of my meditations and continue to employ them without more ado. And the Lord said, "I will cause all my goodness to pass in front of you, and I will proclaim my name, the Lord, in your presence. I will have mercy on whom I will have mercy, and I will have compassion on whom I will have compassion."[3] Just for emphasis it is repeated in Romans 9:15 "I know that everything God does will endure forever; nothing can be added to it, and nothing taken from it. God does it so that people will fear him."[4] Yes, and from ancient days I am he. No one can deliver out of my hand. *When I act, who can reverse it?*"[5] "All the peoples of the earth are regarded as nothing. *He does as he pleases* with the powers of heaven and the peoples of the earth. No one can hold back his hand or say to him: What have you done?"[6] "But I have raised you up for this very purpose, that I might show you my power and that my name might be proclaimed in all the earth."[7] "For from Him and through Him and for Him are all things. To him be the glory forever! Amen."[8] "But who are you, a human being, to talk back to God? "Shall what is formed say to the one who formed it, 'Why did you make me like this? Does not the potter have the right to make out of the same lump of clay some pottery for special purposes and some for common use?"[9]

14

I knew it!! A forked road (such as it is)! Shall we investigate this way for a while and see where it goes or continue in the general direction in which we were going? To be honest there is not much to choose between them at the moment. Shall we not pursue the whole nature of God now and come back to it later, or just take stock of what implications there are for us climbers in what we have just learned. We have only tickled the surface of His selfishness and not even mentioned His wrath so it might be quicker to do the detour first as we will be coming back to this spot anyway. I am now aware that I am having conversations with 'imaginary friends' lol, I am aware that I trek alone but am sure that there will be some who choose to follow me up, I pray that the Lord will bless you and that you will discover Him in a new way whilst on your own trek. I will mark my own way as best I can to make it easier to follow but I do warn you that the navigational aids will not make it easy! By the way did you notice the 'F' word further up? 'fear'; that is going to be a real challenge higher up the mountain- very steep and rocky indeed! Meanwhile is your ego challenged by being considered a mere lump of clay as in Romans 19? So was mine a long time ago; I have heard the argument so many times and presented it myself with a fair degree of antipathy, the question 'do you think that I am just a pawn in a cosmic chess game?' The answer, maybe surprisingly, is yes; sort of, except that the match is already over and for us disciples, we are on the winning side. Not quite as simple as that though. We have been active participants, we have been able exercise our free will to influence the course of the action but, as we are in the process of discussing, God has selfishly 'arranged' things to turn out exactly how He wanted! "And we know that in all things God works for the good of those who love him, who have been called according to his purpose."[10]

As there are so many diversions on this mountain, God's wisdom is crucial in deciding when to take a detour or diversion or to wait and come back to it. Just a short diversion for a minute, we will get back on the original trail in a moment. If God has already decided the outcome of everything and has given us free will, how does it all work? Well, consider the word 'will'; a lot of trawling has not yielded much linguistic analysis of the word 'will' and so I am going to share what the Spirit has revealed to me and back it up in the Berean tradition (and throw some light on Romans 9). While we are considering His selfish nature let us consider His 'directive will', those things which He has ordained *will* happen. We now know that He is all powerful, He is all wise, He is totally selfish, and He is going to have His own way. *The universe is His creation and thus He is entitled to do what He wishes with it* including us! God raised up Pharaoh for His own purposes: "But I have raised you up for this very purpose, that I might show you my power and that my name might be proclaimed in all the earth."[11] "Therefore, hear what the Lord has planned against Edom, what he has purposed against those who live in Tenan. The young of the flock will be dragged away; their pasture will be appalled at their fate."[12] "For I know the plans I have for you, declares the Lord, plans to prosper you and not to harm you, plans to give you hope and a future."[13] *"I make known the end from the beginning, from ancient times, what is still to come.* I say, 'My purpose will stand, and I will do all that I please."[14] "But Necho sent messengers to him, saying, what quarrel is there, king of Judah, between you and me? It is not you I am attacking at this time, but the house with which I am at war. God has told me to hurry; so stop opposing God, who is with me, or he will destroy you."[15]

"Paul and his companions travelled throughout the region of Phrygia and Galatia, having been kept by the Holy Spirit from preaching the word in the province of Asia."[16] "Now an angel of the Lord said to Philip, Go south to the road, the desert road that goes down from Jerusalem to Gaza."[17] "Cornelius stared at him in fear. What is it, Lord? he asked. The angel answered, your prayers and gifts to the poor have come up as a memorial offering before God. Now send men to Joppa to bring back a man named Simon who is called Peter."[18] "Then the Lord said to Moses, "Go up this mountain in the Abarim Range and see the land I have given the Israelites." Now His permissive will is different, He introduces the factor of our free will, often His promises are only met on condition of our exercising of it in accordance with His approbated will; I use this term in the sense that this is what He would have *preferred* as an alternative, but not a substitute, the more general usage as being deemed 'valid' or 'authorised'

Let us retrace our steps to a topic which arose on the lower slopes; why does all this bad stuff happen? "Let everyone be subject to the governing authorities, for there is no authority except that which God has established."[20] We can all exercise our free will and God can exercise His directive or His permissive will. The authorities that exist have been established by God. (Other translations:- instituted, placed there, under orders, ordained, set up, appointed). But what about those who have ended up in places of authority out of the exercise of the free will of fellow men? Not there by the directive will of God nor realising His approbated will but because of His permissive will. Genghis Khan, Caligula, Hitler, and Idi Armin to name but a few. It has been said that we get the government we deserve. This is not a new revelation "So all the elders of Israel gathered together and came to Samuel at Ramah. They said to him, 'you are old, and your sons do not follow your ways; now appoint a king to lead us, such as all the other nations have.' but when they said 'give us a king to lead us,' this displeased Samuel; so, he prayed to the Lord and the Lord told him: 'Listen to all that the people are saying to you; it is not you they have rejected, but they have rejected me as their king."[21] Look who they got- Saul! and, by and large it all went downhill after that! Leadership is very dangerous ground, and we are not high enough up the mountain to contemplate the topic at the moment, but I pray that this sojourn has provoked some serious thoughts.

Just a short further discussion on the topic of the various aspects of God's will which I pray will help locate the way to the top, or close to it. Let us take a look at Israel at the time of Jeremiah around 627 BC. Israel, the Northern Kingdom had already been dispersed by the Assyrians, for the same reason that Judah was about to be taken into exile; namely they had forsaken the God of Abraham, Isaac, and Jacob. Except for a few short intervals, they had taken to worshipping other gods, they were able to do this because they were free to exercise their free will; they took advantage of God's *permissive* will. His *approbated* will was that they should have kept on worshipping Him, but they didn't!

I am going to quote a fair old chunk of Jeremiah now (see how relevant the older testament is? You cannot afford to try and do without it or ignore the bits you don't like or understand). "Hear the word of the Lord, you descendants of Jacob, all you clans of Israel. This is what the Lord says: 'What fault did your ancestors find in me, that they strayed so far from me? They followed worthless idols and became worthless themselves. They did not ask, 'Where is the Lord, who brought us up out of Egypt and led us through the barren wilderness, through a land of deserts and ravines, a land of drought and utter darkness, a land where no one travels, and no one lives? I brought you into a fertile land to eat its fruit and rich produce. But you came and defiled my land and made my inheritance detestable. The priests did not ask, 'Where is the Lord?' Those who deal with the law did not know me; the leaders rebelled against me. The prophets prophesied by Baal, following worthless idols. 'Therefore, I bring charges against you again,' declares the Lord. 'And I will bring charges against your children's children.'"[22] See? I told you He is a selfish God and remember-*He does not change*! By the way, does any of this part of Jeremiah's prophesy sound familiar? The priests did not ask "Where is the Lord", and the prophets prophesied by Baal! - really whoever heard of such a thing?! Have you heard 'prophets' who always tell you what you want to hear? Have you studied authentic prophets, their messages, and their fates? Well back to Jeremiah again. "Therefore, the Lord Almighty says this: 'Because you have not listened to my words, I will summon all the peoples of the north and my servant Nebuchadnezzar king of Babylon' declares the Lord, 'and I will bring them against this land and its inhabitants and against all the surrounding nations. I will completely destroy them and make them an object of horror and scorn, and an everlasting ruin. I will banish from them the sounds of joy and gladness, the voices of bride and bridegroom, the sound of millstones and the light of the lamp. This whole country will become a desolate wasteland, and these nations will serve the king of Babylon seventy years. But when the seventy years are fulfilled, I will punish the king of Babylon and his nation, the land of the Babylonians, for their guilt,' declares the Lord, 'and will make it desolate forever.'"[23] Now this is the *directive* will of God, it didn't go the way He would have preferred but He got His own way anyway, eventually! But having used the king for His own ends he dealt with him as severely as anyone; that is our enigmatic God at work- get used to it!

Quite a lot of exploration but not a lot of progress upwards, I think. I am pretty sure I will be trudging about on the same patch of mountain for a while; still, I am sure some vertical progress will be made, but it is all down to the directive will of the Father. I follow the example of Jeshua:- "I only do what I see the Father doing."[24] No more, no less! My free spiritual gift for today.

CHAPTER 4

OOPS – THE FIRST SLIPPERY BIT, I THINK; A WORD ABOUT PROPHETS AND WORDS

Who climbs a mountain without an objective? In the case of a physical mountain that objective, presumably, would be just to reach the summit; it has been said that some mountaineers when asked why they wanted to climb it have replied "because it is there". What about a spiritual mountain? Would you choose to climb it just because it is there? Many have but they have chosen mountains which have no summit; they are deluded into believing that they have achieved something but, as there is no summit, they have no real means of evaluating their degree of success or otherwise. This sort of spiritual mountain is assailed by those who think it is a path to some god or other; often the climb is sustained with the use of hallucinogens, bodily self-abuse or mind-altering practices. There is no summit because there is no-one to occupy it-only delusions and occult beings, there is no god. This mountain is different; it is unique because it is the *only* one inhabited by *the* living God with whom we are able to have a personal relationship! No other 'religion' offers the way to a personal, viable relationship with the living God! You cannot have a conversation with a Buddha, you cannot have a conversation with Allah, you cannot have a conversation with Baal, you cannot have a conversation with Zeus, Isis, Odin, or any of the myriad of gods that proliferate the minds of lost mankind. This is a bold statement indeed. Yes, I will introduce the Scriptures in my endorsement of said statement but first a 'muse' or two.

First, I pose a question: - If (and there is) there is a God and He created everything and does all the sorts of stuff we have discussed already (and a lot more to come), what sort of God would He be if He couldn't, wouldn't, or just didn't communicate with us? Apart from the fact that, as we shall discover further up, He created us to have fellowship with Him; without communication we would remain in total ignorance of Him except that we should see Him in His creation. "For since the creation of the world God's invisible qualities, his eternal power and divine nature, have been clearly seen, being understood from what has been made, so that people are without excuse."[1] If He remained incommunicado surely, we should consider Him deficient or impotent in some degree? But that is not the case! Under the New Covenant He communicates with us, His disciples, in all manner of ways and all the time. Under the Old Covenant He selected certain men and women to whom He would speak directly with the charge that they should pass on His statements to the people. These individuals were known as prophets.

Now another diversion whilst some truths are shared about prophets and prophesy. The linguistics of the term 'prophet' are complex; it is foolhardy to adopt a particular idea of the function or calling of the prophet to be sacrosanct. What is certain is that the term has a number of roots; from the Hebrew comes the term 'fruit of the lips'; and from the Greek 'forespeaker' an equivalent of the Hebrew for 'mouthpiece, spokesman, or 'announcer'. According to the Talmud (and who else should we consult but the Jews?) there were hundreds of thousands of prophets and fifty-five recognised Scriptural prophets based on the Talmud and the Rashi; these include Abraham, Isaac, Jacob, Moses, Aaron, Gad, David, Solomon, Jonah, Uriah, Sarah, Deborah, and Hannah.

Interestingly Daniel is not to be a considered a prophet, the contention is that the Word the Lord gave him was not intended to be spoken out to the people but to be written down for future generations. That is why it is included in the 'writings' portion of the Scriptures rather than the 'prophets'. There is no qualification or prerequisite to fulfil the role of prophet! You cannot be taught 'how to do it' there is no 'training program' the prophet is called directly by God and *never* appointed by man- contrary to a lot of garbage teaching being propagated today.

Romans 11:29 tells us that "God's gifts and his call are irrevocable." The role of prophet is a gift and a call from God through the Holy Spirit. I guarantee that none of the prophets recognised by anyone with spiritual credibility ever went on a course, read a 'how to' book or watched a DVD! Any references to a 'school' of prophets are invalid it does not appear anywhere in the Scriptures. Anyone, maybe everyone, may be called upon to fulfil the role, although it is not uncommon for someone to prophesy and not be aware of the role they are fulfilling. *Any* word spoken by an individual under the anointing of the Holy Spirit is prophesy. (a prophesy is what is spoken on behalf of God by a prophet- surprisingly- not necessarily a prediction for the future) This includes a word of knowledge, a word of wisdom, a word for healing or a word for deliverance or a word for anything else; if God speaks to you through the Holy Spirit and you are told to speak it out you have been given a prophesy and you are fulfilling the role of prophet. It is not a status; it is a function distributed throughout the body of Christ by the Holy Spirit and widely employed by Him. I think as we will have to consider the 'word' of God briefly as I consider the Scriptures to be the word of God and I am trying to present the case for my using them as immutable evidence in the course of my musings. This is an issue which causes a multitude of problems because of lack of wise teaching. Bearing in mind the advice Paul gave to Timothy: "Keep reminding God's people of these things. Warn them before God against quarrelling about words; it is of no value, and only ruins those who listen."[2]

This is going to be the first section of the climb where the going gets steep and slippery, maybe skating on thin ice but, as always, I shall apply Berean principles. There is so much discourse on the interpretation of the word 'word' that it is impossible to apply academic and analytical principles in trying to arrive at any conclusion. This is because in the Greek there are basically two words translated 'word':- logos and rhema. The consensus is that rhema applies only to an utterance, something which is 'spoken out' and both are used in translating from the Hebrew 'dabar'. Logos is used in other senses of the 'word' such as "In the beginning was the Word, and the Word was with God, and the Word was God."[3] and "This is the meaning of the parable: The seed is the word of God."[4] So this is a right can of worms! A perfect state in which the wisdom of God is demonstrated to be essential in discerning what He wants to make known to us through His Spirit and it is vital for the disciple to have an understanding of this absolute truth. What cannot be determined by fleshy analysis and human logic can be understood through the wisdom of the Holy Spirit. This is one of the functions of the prophet- so here goes! What is certain is that there are two (mainly) singularly different manifestations of a word. First the word which is spoken- breathed out- of an individual and received by direct communication with one or more other individuals. Then the word which is disseminated by other means:- letter, radio, Newspaper, email, flyer etc. This word may or may not have its origin in a particular individual who is being quoted word for word. If you are in love with someone is having 'sweet nothings' whispered in your ear the same as getting a text or email? No! of course not, the two are entirely different. So 'word' has two distinct connotations. The essential difference is that the authenticity and integrity of the rhema (I will use this term in this respect from now on) cannot be denied whereas this does not necessarily apply to the logos; the origin of logos is never absolutely determinable except when verified by the determinant of the logos itself. Sorry, there is no way to make this simpler, I don't think. Anyway, hopefully, it is now easy to see that an individual may deliver a speech (rhema) which a secretary may record verbatim or may record on a DVD- whatever! But it is no longer rhema it is now logos. If the originator of the statement then reads it out, it becomes rhema- direct from the horse's mouth, even if he said it once (or more) already. They are distinct and different.

An understanding of this distinction is crucial, and I will explain why. Let us consider 2 Corinthians 3:6:- "He has made us competent as ministers of a new covenant, not of the letter but of the Spirit; for the letter kills, but the Spirit gives life." "Now an angel of the Lord said to Philip, "Go south to the road, the desert road that goes down from Jerusalem to Gaza. So he started out, and on his way he met an Ethiopian eunuch, an important official in charge of all the treasury of the Kandake (which means "queen of the Ethiopians"). This man had gone to Jerusalem to worship, and, on his way home, was sitting in his chariot reading the Book of Isaiah the prophet. The Spirit told Philip, "Go to that chariot and stay near it." Then Philip ran up to the chariot and heard the man reading Isaiah the prophet. "Do you understand what you are reading?" Philip asked. "How can I," he said, "unless someone explains it to me?" So he invited Philip to come up and sit with him. This is the passage of Scripture the eunuch was reading: "He was led like a sheep to the slaughter, and as a lamb before its shearer is silent, so he did not open his mouth. In his humiliation he was deprived of justice. Who can speak of his descendants? For his life was taken from the earth." The eunuch asked Philip, "Tell me, please, who is the prophet talking about, himself or someone else?" Then Philip began with that very passage of Scripture and told him the good news about Jesus. As they travelled along the road, they came to some water and the eunuch said, "Look, here is water. What can stand in the way of my being baptized?" And Philip said, "If you believe with all your heart, you may." And he answered and said, "I believe that Jesus Christ is the Son of God." And he gave orders to stop the chariot. Then both Philip and the eunuch went down into the water and Philip baptized him."[5] The eunuch was reading the Torah (logos) he, like millions of others who have read the Scriptures (logos) had no idea what they were reading, it was only when he encountered (Spirit filled) Philip that the logos became rhema and brought him life! Let us see what Jeshua had to offer on the topic:- "He said to them, "This is what I told you while I was still with you: Everything must be fulfilled that is written about me in the Law of Moses, the Prophets, and the

Psalms. Then he opened their minds so they could understand the Scriptures."[6] Jeshua, of course, was the word (logos) made flesh *and* the word (rhemata) of God.

The scribes, Pharisees and Sadducees were all highly accomplished scholars and had been for generations; they knew the Scriptures inside out, many of them could quote vast portions of the Tanakh and the Torah verbatim. Corporately they had taken what was meant by God to be advice on how to live a productive and fruitful life and debased it into a self-gratifying legalistic system. "Jesus replied, "You are in error because you do not know the Scriptures or the power of God."[7] Jeshua was quoted by Satan in the wilderness. Yes, he knows them all backwards and still tries to seduce Christians with them, and he does not, necessarily, misquote them as is often contended. He can accurately quote large selections out of context or without reference to the whole of Scripture, contrary to the Berean principle, a technique also applied by many cults. Millions have read and heard enough of Scripture sufficient for salvation but remained lost, only because they have not had their minds opened by the Holy Spirit. There is even a sin known as bibliolatry, bible worship; it is a sin because insofar as it is not under any anointing of the Holy Spirit as in the case of the religious of Yeshua's day, Satan, and the cults, it is logos and only another book. There is a significant reference in 2 Corinthians 3:6, "He has made us competent as ministers of a new covenant, not of the letter but of the Spirit; *for the letter kills*, but the Spirit gives life." The word translated 'letter' is 'grammatos'; grammata are best interpreted in this instance as 'empty words'- just words. Father wants us to talk to Him and not just read another book. Yes, He does want us to study His Word but not at the expense of time sitting at His feet listening. Is it easier to spend an hour basically composing a commentary or an hour on your face before the throne of glory?

Let us see exactly what Scripture has to say about itself. Here is a good one to start: - "All Scripture is God-breathed and is useful for teaching, rebuking, correcting, and training in righteousness."[8] N.B. Bible school graduates and bibliolaters; *not* essential, loads of people have been saved whilst nowhere near a bible and in some cases never having been near one! Only essential, I guess, if you are a Berean (I need an emocion here- a smiley face and a hand held up). Back to the case in hand! "He humbled you, causing you to hunger and then feeding you with manna, which neither you nor your ancestors had known, to teach you that man does not live on bread alone but on every word that comes from the mouth of the Lord"[9] "As the rain and the snow come down from heaven, and do not return to it without watering the earth and making it bud and flourish, so that it yields seed for the sower and bread for the eater, so is my word that goes out from my mouth: It will not return to me empty, *but will accomplish what I desire and achieve the purpose for which I sent it.*"[10]

"Every word of God is flawless; he is a shield to those who take refuge in him. Do not add to his words, or he will rebuke you and prove you a liar"[11] "The grass withers and the flowers fall, but the word of our God endures forever."[12] "See that you do all I command you; do not add to it or take away from it."[13] Jeshua said that Scripture cannot be altered[14] "The Spirit gives life; the flesh counts for nothing. The words I have spoken to you, they are full of the Spirit and life."[15] From Romans 15:4 scripture tells us:- "For everything that was written in the past was written to teach us, so that through the endurance taught in the Scriptures and the encouragement they provide we might have hope." "For the word of God is alive and active. Sharper than any double-edged sword, it penetrates even to dividing soul and spirit, joints, and marrow; it judges the thoughts and attitudes of the heart."[16] "For prophecy never had its origin in the human will, but prophets, though human, spoke from God as they were carried along by the Holy Spirit."[17] "He writes the same way in all his letters, speaking in them of these matters. His letters contain some things that are hard to understand, which ignorant and unstable people distort as they do the other Scriptures, to their own destruction."[18] A virus rampant in today's church because the admonition not to leave any of it (scripture) out is ignored. Final word from the Saviour:- "For truly I tell you, until heaven and earth disappear, not the smallest letter, not the least stroke of a pen, will by any means disappear from the Law until everything is accomplished."[19]

Wow! a bit of a longer trek this time I knew the going was going to get harder, so it is no surprise. Not a place I would have chosen to stop and make camp, but we are where we are PTL! I am expecting that the next part of the trek will reveal a degree of convergence of the various detours and exploratory trips that have been made but we shall all have to wait and see what Father has in mind! In the meantime, I wish all my beloved brothers and sisters every blessing and, if there are any unbelievers attempting the climb, I wish you God speed.

CHAPTER 5

And Now For Something Entirely Different: - Of Navigation and Inspiration

Perhaps it is appropriate, sometimes, to stop, ponder and meditate upon how much progress (or otherwise) one might be making on such an undertaking as this. I am not inclined to strive upwards and onwards at the moment; I am more inclined to consider what has been accomplished so far. To be honest we are not far up the mountain, there is still a long way to go, and the way ahead is arduous, that was acknowledged to be the case before we even started. Shall I retrace some steps that have been taken, re-evaluate and elaborate upon them? Shall I plod on for a while (as has already been deliberated) then come back? Or shall I plot, more accurately if I can, the route we have taken so far?

Before GPS was widely employed for navigation, we used a system called D.R. (dead reckoning) by the judicious use of sundry cunning devices, we could figure out, purely through the amazing skills known as observation, data acquisition and mathematics, where we were, to a given degree of accuracy. Having calculated this postulated position subject to the n'th degree of accuracy, we would then choose a theoretical position on the chart which represented our most precarious position in real life. The same principles might be applied to an undertaking such as this. Perhaps more ground has been covered than was first assumed, there has been no real effort to make progress upward for a while so I have spent time assessing what progress might have been made before pressing on. To this end I have re-read the earlier missives and have decided it is appropriate to summarise the ground covered. Using scripture as the sole source of reliable witness and applying Berean principles to its employment and value as evidence the following truths have been established God does not change; corollary:- the *whole* of scripture is totally relevant. Gods' wisdom is beyond our understanding; corollary:- our wisdom is foolishness to Him.

Such wisdom as we have is sourced *only* from the Holy Spirit. Corollary:- we have to put our fleshy wisdom to death on the cross before we can have authentic Godly understanding, The Hellenistic mindset is a killer.

- God is infallible and His plan is perfect.
- God is *entitled* to behave anyway He wishes.
- The *only* definition of a disciple is that they should have given up everything.
- Our Lord only asks for love and obedience.
- God is utterly selfish and does exactly as He pleases.
- The infallibility of the scriptures has not been fully discussed yet- might come back to that one as we start up the slope again.
- There are three aspects to His will; His directive will, His permissive will and His approbated will.
- There are two main words in English translated from original languages which have distinctly different meanings but are both translated as 'word'.
- A prophet is anyone who hears God speak to him/her on a personal and empirical level who is then commanded to share that word with others, this constitutes a prophesy.
- The scriptures under the anointing of the Holy Spirit are the infallible and complete revelation of God.

Well yes, so we have covered a bit more ground than was anticipated and have exposed a need to 'nail down' the case for the infallibility of the scriptures. Stepping out of the spiritual realm briefly and resorting to systems of reasoned argument and logic, consider the following. First some definitions so that we are absolutely clear, for the purposes of our study, exactly what we are talking about.

1) A premise is a statement which can be taken as read, already accepted as true either because it is blatantly true and needs no proof or has been demonstrated to be true experimentally.
2) A proposition is a statement which may or may not be true and is open for discussion with a view to determining its truth or falsehood.
3) An argument is not a heated difference of opinion but a logical tool by means of which a proposition may be rendered true or false.

Now the argument: - *if* there exists a deity as described in the scriptures as being the God of Abraham, Isaac, and Jacob; *then* He should be able to communicate with His creation on a personal level. The question is this, is it the case that He cannot, will not, or just does not? or does He? Unless one is totally atheistic, which is totally illogical in itself as there is absolutely no system of reasoned argument that can endorse the proposition that 'there is no God', (thereby the statement is rendered inane) then the question posed is worthy of debate. Considering that Darwinian evolution is being discredited on a daily basis due to the fact that its argument is basically flawed on a number of counts, a fact which is becoming more and more acknowledged by many of its adherents including some notoriously well-known ones, and that creation, AKA 'the big bang' is now totally accepted, then the proposition that 'God communicates with us on a personal level' is worthy of argument.

As a premise I state that "Having created all of heaven and earth and all that there is therein, He had a reason for doing so. That He did not do it just for something to do because He was fed up playing heavenly bingo or even multi-dimensional chess! He created it all and us because He was lonely, He wanted us to love and be loved because He made us in His image."

30

Now- the proposal that He *cannot* is reduced to absurdity based on this premise. Maybe He will not; this is often the case as it was with many pagan cultures and often His own people. Maybe He just does not; this is part of my testimony as is the fact that often He *does* speak to us, I know when He speaks to me and so do millions of others throughout the nations and throughout time. Perhaps we will discuss how I know another time but for today this is my testimony. He has spoken to individuals throughout the whole of history, from Adam and Eve in Genesis to John of Patmos in Revelation. Not so many in the older testament but thousands in the newer testament and millions and millions since.

As has been established that, when God speaks to a person that person assumes, for the time being, the role of prophet, and if, as part of what is revealed that person is told to make God's word known to others that becomes a prophesy. Nothing necessarily, though possibly, to do with foretelling the future! Sometimes, as is the case here, the prophet is told to record the prophesy; sometimes, as is the case with some of the older testament prophets, others were commissioned to record what was said on their behalf. The same happens today with the use of recording devices and media. To re-iterate, the word of God as breathed by Him into the empirical experience of the prophet by the power of the Holy Spirit is what the Greeks referred to as the rhema, God-breathed word. The recording of that rhema becomes logos, the same words verbatim but without the breath of God in them until the Holy Spirit breathes that same life into them for the particular benefit of the individual reading them or hearing them. That is why we are told by the scriptures themselves that "the letter kills but the Spirit brings life."[1] It is not, as some contend, a reference to the Law because that has never changed! It is an admonition to the preachers of the Gospel to preach under the anointing of the Holy Spirit. A few more premises:- we know that Satan knows the whole of scripture verbatim, if you have not had whole chunks of scripture quoted at you by the enemy and you become an effective disciple of Christ- you will! Cults of all sorts, shapes and sizes use tracts of scripture for their own ends. (This is another vitally important reason for always applying the Berean principle always use the *whole* of scripture for guidance, not just the bits you can cope with.) We know that we are going to be subject to deceit and false prophesy, check out some 'Christian' TV channels and literature, all use swathes of 'sound' biblical teaching– *until* you study it in the light of the *whole* of scripture.

Many, many people have read bibles over and over and not found Christ because they have been under the influences of spirits other than His Holiness, the Holy Spirit, If they had read their scripture with ears sensitive to the God-breathed word, then at least they would have been convicted and likely found salvation. Many would spend their (and God's) time more profitably being still and knowing that He is God, rather than spouting volumes of scripture at poor, unsuspecting, long-suffering congregations who think it would be unholy to avoid the tedium. I quote Jeshua Himself as recorded by John: -" You study the Scriptures diligently because you think that in them you have eternal life. These are the very Scriptures that testify about me, yet you refuse to come to me to have life."[2] Just a word for the dissenters and bibliolaters; Just remember that millions have been saved without a bible in sight, and often never has been. Consider what the scriptures say about themselves. "All Scripture is God-breathed and is useful for teaching, rebuking, correcting and training in righteousness."[3] Note! All translation is either 'useful' or 'profitable', none essential! But let us start at the beginning reading the rhema by God's grace under the anointing of the Holy Spirit. "He humbled you, causing you to hunger and then feeding you with manna, which neither you nor your ancestors had known, to teach you that man does not live on bread alone but on every word that comes from the mouth of the Lord."[4] The word which comes from the mouth of the Lord. "Do not add to what I command you and do not subtract from it but keep the commands of the Lord your God that I give you."[5] 'Do not add or take away from it' is repeated, for emphasis, later during the sojourn of the Israelites in the desert[6] "Special notice for those who leave out huge chunks for fear of causing offence!

"The grass withers and the flowers fall, *but the word of our God endures forever.*"[7] "As the rain and the snow come down from heaven, and do not return to it without watering the earth and making it bud and flourish, so that it yields seed for the sower and bread for the eater, so is my word that goes out from my mouth: It will not return to me empty, but *will accomplish what I desire and achieve the purpose for which I sent it.*"[8] Note well; God's perfect and infallible plan! "Is not my word like fire," declares the Lord, "and like a hammer that breaks a rock in pieces?"[9] And still relevant today "For the word of God is alive and active. Sharper than any double-edged sword, it penetrates even to dividing soul and spirit, joints and marrow; it judges the thoughts and attitudes of the heart."[10] Words of wisdom from Joshua "Keep this Book of the Law always on your lips; meditate on it day and night, so that you may be careful to do everything written in it. Then you will be prosperous and successful."[11] This is one of God's conditional promises, an example of His approbated will.

A treasure from the Psalms "The law of the Lord is perfect, refreshing the soul. The statutes of the Lord are trustworthy, making wise the simple. The precepts of the Lord are right, giving joy to the heart. The commands of the Lord are radiant, giving light to the eyes. The fear of the Lord is pure, enduring forever. The decrees of the Lord are firm, and all of them are righteous. They are more precious than gold, than much pure gold; they are sweeter than honey, than honey from the honeycomb. By them your servant is warned; in keeping them there is great reward."[12] "I desire to do your will, my God; your law is within my heart." Said King David.[13] And from proverbs:- "Every word of God is flawless; he is a shield to those who take refuge in him. Do not add to his words, or he will rebuke you and prove you a liar."[14] Some reflective notes from the newer testament concerning the testimony of the scriptures regarding themselves. "For everything that was written in the past was written to teach us, so that through the endurance taught in the Scriptures and the encouragement they provide we might have hope."[15] "Above all, you must understand that no prophecy of Scripture came about by the prophet's own interpretation of things, for prophecy never had its origin in the human will, but prophets, though human, spoke from God as they were carried along by the Holy Spirit."[16] "But *the word of the Lord endures forever.* And this is the word that was preached to you."[17] "His divine power has given us everything we need for a godly life through our knowledge of him who called us by his own glory and goodness. Through these he has given us his very great and precious promises, so that through them you may participate in the divine nature, having escaped the corruption in the world caused by evil desires."[18]

A few verses to sum up. "And we also thank God continually because, when you received the word of God, which you heard from us, you accepted it not as a human word, but as it actually is, the word of God, which is indeed at work in you who believe."[19] Jeshua said "The Spirit gives life; the flesh counts for nothing. The words I have spoken to you, they are full of the Spirit and life."[20] Words of the flesh count for nothing how much breath are you wasting? "Bear in mind that our Lord's patience means salvation, just as our dear brother Paul also wrote you with the wisdom that God gave him. He writes the same way in all his letters, speaking in them of these matters. His letters contain some things that are hard to understand, which ignorant and unstable people distort, as they do the other Scriptures, to their own destruction."[21] "I warn everyone who hears the words of the prophecy of this scroll: If anyone adds anything to them, God will add to that person the plagues described in this scroll. And if anyone takes words away from this scroll of prophecy, God will take away from that person any share in the tree of life and in the Holy City, which are described in this scroll."[22]

I conclude that the Holy Spirit, in this case employing some of the principles of reasoned argument, has made His case for ascribing infallibility to the scriptures with regard to the legitimacy of accepting them as the word (rhema) of God; thus, rendering them appropriate for teaching, rebuking, correcting, and training. They are utterances made by God to individuals throughout time and have been recorded, as they themselves state, for the purposes quoted. Being statements having been made by God they are, in themselves, infallible but in their recorded state are merely logos until breathed upon anew by the Holy Spirit for the fulfilling of Gods purposes with regard to an, or a group of, other individual(s). And, as again stated in themselves, particularly by Jeshua, without the Holy Spirit their truth and validity will not be acknowledged. I now consider my claims regarding the scriptures to have been validated and will continue up the mountain on that basis. I know that I am sharing the word (rhema) of the Lord and that as I disseminate that word it will be of no value to some but will be of great value to at least one, otherwise He would not have had me spend time on it, He will breathe life back into the logos and blessing will flow. I re-quote:- "The word of the Lord does not go forth and return void." I pray for the Spirit to be on everyone who reads this, and that they should go forth with joy.

CHAPTER 6

A SHEER FACE AND THE 'F' WORD - FEAR (AND TREPIDATION!)

Fear. Hmm. When did you last (or ever) give any thought to the fact that the scriptures cite 'the fear of God' 84 times, 'fear of God' 86 times, 'fear the Lord' 186 times and 'fear God' 134 times; total 490 times! 239 times 'terror' is used often in relation to the effect that God has on wayward humanity. I will just quote one from Deuteronomy; "So the Lord brought us out of Egypt with a mighty hand and an outstretched arm, *with great terror* and with signs and wonders."[1] You can look all the others up yourselves- why should I do all the work? Before going further, I will restate two important established facts:- 1) God does not change! 2) we are in no position to query or challenge His decisions!

Before really engaging in the next part of the climb we have to contemplate one of the hazards on the way. We acknowledge a triune God, God the Father, God the Son, and God the Holy Spirit. We also acknowledge that they are also the *one* true God. Our first paradox (and there will be more because our God is, by nature, paradoxical) is that God's wisdom is utterly beyond our understanding. We are lumbered with a tripartite *and* singular God. We have to accept it at get on with it! If we want to become theological in the academic sense, we might argue that the triune nature of God is demonstrated in the older testament testifying to the nature of the Father, the newer testament testifying to the nature of the Son and both testaments testifying, in varying degrees, to the Holy Spirit. I would not be foolish enough to endorse such an opinion, but the case is plausible I will concede. However, it is time to put on the crampons and harness and begin the climb, we will first consider the expectations of our forefather Abraham. "Abraham replied, "I said to myself, 'There is surely no fear of God in this place, and they will kill me because of my wife."[2] It is pretty clear that Abraham had an expectation that the king and inhabitants of Gerar would 'fear' God. This is not a linguistic issue, 'fear' is the literal translation used in every case (20+ translations); definitions include 'terror',' dread', 'awe', 'reverence' 'trepidation' and 'consternation'. The corollary is that he had this expectation because this was his own testimony regarding God's dealings with him. This man, aged 75, ups sticks, and trundles off into the unknown, only on the word of God. He must have experienced every one of those definitions of 'fear' and all 40-odd others. More persuasive is the episode recorded in Genesis:- "Do not lay a hand on the boy," he said. "Do not do anything to him. Now I know that you fear God, because you have not withheld from me your son, your only son."[3]

A little aside here; if you are puzzled as to why God needed to know that Abraham feared Him because God already knows everything, then consider that it was more likely that it was Abraham who needed to know how much he feared his God. Maybe some translation matters here or just Holy Spirit inspiration. Later Joseph expressed he same sentiment, "On the third day, Joseph said to them, "Do this and you will live, for I fear God." Moses encountered the same issue with Pharaoh, "But I know that you and your officials still do not fear the Lord God."[5] Egypt and Israel were to soon learn how apt, proper and seemly it is to literally 'fear' the Lord.

After all the plagues that had already been inflicted upon the Egyptians "At midnight the Lord struck down all the firstborn in Egypt, from the firstborn of Pharaoh, who sat on the throne, to the firstborn of the prisoner, who was in the dungeon, and the firstborn of all the livestock as well."[6] It seems that the awful truth had not sunk in, and Egypt would pay the ultimate price for their contempt and stupidity:-" Moses stretched out his hand over the sea, and at daybreak the sea went back to its place. The Egyptians were fleeing toward it, and the Lord swept them into the sea."[7] That, in itself, would, and does, make me very fearful of the Living God; but there is more!

It was not long before Israel forgot and opted for the golden calf with the consequence that God ordered the death of three thousand of His chosen people. "Then he said to them, "This is what the Lord, the God of Israel, says: 'Each man strap a sword to his side. Go back and forth through the camp from one end to the other, each killing his brother and friend and neighbour. The Levites did as Moses commanded, and that day about three thousand of the people died."[8] Israel was commanded four times in Leviticus to fear their God and several times in Deuteronomy. Let us review how God dealt with some of Israel's enemies:- The Amorites: "As they fled before Israel on the road down from Beth Horon to Azekah, the Lord hurled large hailstones down on them, and more of them died from the hail than were killed by the swords of the Israelites. On the day the Lord gave the Amorites over to Israel, Joshua said to the Lord in the presence of Israel: "Sun, stand still over Gibeon, and you, moon, over the Valley of Aijalon. So the sun stood still, and the moon stopped, till the nation avenged itself on its enemies, as it is written in the Book of Jashar. The sun stopped in the middle of the sky and delayed going down about a full day."[9] Wow! That must have been pretty terrifying!

The Midianites: "When the three hundred trumpets sounded, the Lord caused the men throughout the camp to turn on each other with their swords. The army fled to Beth Shittah toward Zererah as far as the border of Abel Meholah near Tabbath."[10]

The Philistines: "Then Samuel took a suckling lamb and sacrificed it as a whole burnt offering to the Lord. He cried out to the Lord on Israel's behalf, and the Lord answered him. While Samuel was sacrificing the burnt offering, the Philistines drew near to engage Israel in battle. But that day the Lord thundered with loud thunder against the Philistines and threw them into such a panic that they were routed before the Israelites. The men of Israel rushed out of Mizpah and pursued the Philistines, slaughtering them along the way to a point below Beth Kar."[11]

The Assyrians: "That night the angel of the Lord went out and put to death a hundred and eighty-five thousand in the Assyrian camp. When the people got up the next morning there were all the dead bodies!"[12]

What about His dealings with His own chosen people, Israel? "You (Jeroboam) have done more evil than all who lived before you. You have made for yourself other gods, idols made of metal; you have aroused my anger and turned your back on me. Because of this, I am going to bring disaster on the house of Jeroboam. I will cut off from Jeroboam every last male in Israel slave or free. I will burn up the house of Jeroboam as one burns dung, until it is all gone. Dogs will eat those belonging to Jeroboam who die in the city, and the birds will feed on those who die in the country. The Lord has spoken!"[13] The same thing happened to Baasha a few kings later.[14] Let us also have a look at Josiah, an altogether different kind of guy: - "Neither before nor after Josiah was there a king like him who turned to the Lord as he did with all his heart and with all his soul and with all his strength, in accordance with all the Law of Moses. Nevertheless, the Lord did not turn away from the heat of his fierce anger, which burned against Judah because of all that Manasseh had done to arouse his anger."[15] (Other translations use 'wrath').

How did God manifest His wrath? "I will uproot from among you your Asherah poles when I demolish your cities. *I will take vengeance in anger and wrath on the nations that have not obeyed me.*"[16] Micah's prophesy indicates that God's wrath is not soon dissipated;- "Because I have sinned against him, I will bear the Lord's wrath, until he pleads my case and upholds my cause. He will bring me out into the light; I will see his righteousness"[17] This proved later to be the case. "By the wrath of the Lord Almighty the land will be scorched, and the people will be fuel for the fire; they will not spare one another."[18] "Woe to the Assyrian, the rod of my anger, in whose hand is the club of my wrath! I send him against a godless nation, I dispatch him against a people who anger me, to seize loot and snatch plunder, and to trample them down like mud in the streets."[19] Of course the inevitable outcome was that Israel (Samaria) taken into exile by the Assyrians and dispersed throughout the nations. As for the Southern Kingdom of Judah, did they fare better? "This is what the Sovereign Lord says: "Disaster! Unheard-of disaster! See, it comes! The end has come! The end has come! It has roused itself against you. See, it comes! Doom has come upon you, upon you who dwell in the land. The time has come! The day is near! There is panic, not joy, on the mountains. I am about to pour out my wrath on you and spend my anger against you. I will judge you according to your conduct and repay you for all your detestable practices. I will not look on you with pity; I will not spare you. I will repay you for your conduct and for the detestable practices among you. Then you will know that it is I the Lord who strikes you."[20]

"During Jehoiakim's reign, Nebuchadnezzar king of Babylon invaded the land, and Jehoiakim became his vassal for three years. But then he turned against Nebuchadnezzar and rebelled. The Lord sent Babylonian, Aramean, Moabite, and Ammonite raiders against him to destroy Judah, in accordance with the word of the Lord proclaimed by his servants the prophets. Surely these things happened to Judah according to the Lord's command, in order to remove them from his presence because of the sins of Manasseh and all he had done, including the shedding of innocent blood. For he had filled Jerusalem with innocent blood, and the Lord was not willing to forgive. As for the other events of Jehoiakim's reign, and all he did, are they not written in the book of the annals of the kings of Judah?"[21] You think that is Older Testament and so not relevant? Oh dear!

Mary's reaction on hearing of the baby Baptist leaping in Elizabeth's' womb:- "His mercy extends to those who fear him, from generation to generation."[22] The word 'fear' is the same one used in all translations. Jesus said:- "But I will show you whom you should fear: Fear him who, after your body has been killed, has authority to throw you into hell. Yes, I tell you, fear him."[23] The same word- 3 times! "But when he saw many of the Pharisees and Sadducees coming to where he was baptizing, he said to them: "You brood of vipers! Who warned you to flee from the coming wrath?"[24] Whoever believes in the Son has eternal life, but whoever rejects the Son will not see life, for God's wrath remains on them."[25] From Acts, if it was needed, an example of the relevance of God's wrath:- "Then Peter said, "Ananias, how is it that Satan has so filled your heart that you have lied to the Holy Spirit and have kept for yourself some of the money you received for the land? Didn't it belong to you before it was sold? And after it was sold, wasn't the money at your disposal? What made you think of doing such a thing? You have not lied just to human beings but to God. When Ananias heard this, he fell down and died- (Saphira, his missus, suffered the same fate); and great fear seized all who heard what had happened."[26]

Paul warned the Ephesians:- "Let no one deceive you with empty words, *for because of such things God's wrath comes on those who are disobedient.*"[27] From the letter to the Colossians, "Put to death, therefore, whatever belongs to your earthly nature: sexual immorality, impurity, lust, evil desires and greed, which is idolatry. Because of these, the wrath of God is coming."[27] And to the Thessalonians: -"They displease God and are hostile to everyone in their effort to keep us from speaking to the Gentiles so that they may be saved. In this way they always heap up their sins to the limit. The wrath of God has come upon them at last."[28] Closing, of course, with the words given to John in his Revelation:- "They, too, will drink the wine of God's fury, which has been poured full strength into the cup of his wrath. They will be tormented with burning sulphur in the presence of the holy angels and of the Lamb."[29] "I saw in heaven another great and marvellous sign: seven angels with the seven last plagues, last, because with them God's wrath is completed."[30] "Who will not fear you, Lord, and bring glory to your name? For you alone are holy. All nations will come and worship before you, for your righteous acts have been revealed."[31] "Coming out of his mouth is a sharp sword with which to strike down the nations. "He will rule them with an iron sceptre. He treads the winepress of the fury of the wrath of God Almighty."[32]

All those references to 'fear' and 'wrath' are used in all translations into English and are pertinent to the original languages- consult Strong's concordance. There is no extenuation for changing the language to avoid truths because they violate the 'Santa Claus' image employed and enjoyed by so many 'pavlova' preachers and teachers. I know exactly what charges will be laid: -'this is unbalanced and biased'. This is true, it is unbalanced because the prophesy which has been revealed to us for some time that 'God is sick of a sick church' is so close to my heart that it has been incumbent upon me to redress the imbalance in the other direction that been propagated in pursuit of the 'Santa Claus' model. When have you heard a preacher preach on the wrath of God? When have you heard a teacher teach on the need to hold him in awe and wonder in the manner of the true definition of the words? Do you think this might be bias? Basically, these truths have been part of the gospel (all of it!) from day one. From the time Abraham left Ur of the Chaldees, right through to Jeshua, Paul, and John. What happened?

Well, it seems as though we are halfway up a steep face with two choices, cut the rope and plummet down into the depths from which we started or buckle up and continue the climb. Are you coming? We are going up to confront another paradox. Have you ever considered why God created this universe? Had He got bored and just wanted something to do that week? I think not! From what I know of His character, and we shall be investigating that further shortly; and, in view of His selfishness (which we can modify slightly to self-indulgence), and the fact that:- "we know and rely on the love God has for us. God is love. Whoever lives in love lives in God, and God in them."[33] We might be entitled to speculate a little on His reasons for our being here. The word used by John is agapé, if you do not understand the uniqueness and profound inferences of agapé, please look it up.

Agapé is 'other-centred love.' Agapé incorporates self-sacrifice, total and irrevocable commitment, and an intimacy way beyond that of blood- love which is storge (the natural love which is born out of blood relationships). Love or really close friendship is referred to in scripture as phileo or philia. Agapé love uniquely describes God's love, and employed only once, I believe, outside the scriptures. If God can properly, and He can, be described as agapé, consider His condition. How is He to express Himself? How is He to actually be Himself if there is no-one for Him to agapé? In order to be completely Himself He needed an object of His agapé. What about the angels then? We know from Job 38:7ff that He created the angels before the universe. "Where were you when I laid the earth's foundation? Tell me, if you understand, who marked off its dimensions? Surely you know! Who stretched a measuring line across it? On what were its footings set, or who laid its cornerstone while the morning stars sang together, and all the angels shouted for joy?"

We also know that something went, apparently, awry; Satan fell from heaven and Jeshua saw it "I saw Satan fall like lightning from heaven."[34] Now God is omniscient, so He knew what was going to happen beforehand. What is going on? I conjecture that Father was preparing the way for the fall of man, really? - yes why not? We have already established His selfish nature! In order for Him to express His agapé He had to be in a position to make that self-sacrificial statement and He chose to do it through the redemption of fallen man. We do not know why he did not choose to redeem the fallen angels; we do not really know anything of the character of angels, but we can conclude, legitimately, I think, that they were not the most appropriate objects of His agapé- in His judgement anyway. Perhaps they had not been given absolute free will, and rebellion in the heavenlies was unredeemable. We do know that Jeshua said "And so I tell you, every kind of sin and slander can be forgiven, but blasphemy against the Spirit will not be forgiven."[35] However we are now at the place where we might be getting a glimpse of where the next paradox rears its head, I am inclined to take a breather before pressing on.

CHAPTER 7

OH DEAR! - CONCERNING OBEDIENCE AND SACRIFICE

Yes, we are heading straight up towards a paradox, *but* I have a few observations and some ways of approaching it which might help to 'circumnavigate' it, as it were. Let us pursue the concept of agapé a bit further. In the midst of all of God's terrible dealings with His creation we are able to discern other aspects of His character which give rise to the paradox which we are about to face. Let us first consider the words of Paul "The law was brought in so that the trespass might increase. But where sin increased, grace increased all the more."[1] Since the fall of man which occurred, remember, almost as soon as we stepped foot on the planet; God has had to contend with the fact that He, in all His glory and holiness, has chosen to accommodate His defiled creation. Now we had been created to satisfy His agapé but instead we violated it. Back to basics:- He is utterly selfish, and absolutely entitled to indulge Himself. When we did not fulfil His approbated will (that which He would *preferred* to have happened) He got very, very angry- not just 'throw the dollies out of the pram' angry, but absolutely mind- blowingly, categorically, and devastatingly furious, as is His right, as we have established. So, He is justified in His behaviour, we might not like it, we might not approve of or condone it, *we might resent it or rail against it, but is done and dusted!* The Law was already established before any of it was given to humanity, the Law epitomises agapé- "On one occasion an expert in the law stood up to test Jesus. "Teacher," he asked, "what must I do to inherit eternal life?"[2] "What is written in the Law?" he replied.

"How do you read it?" He answered, "Love the Lord your God with all your heart and with all your soul and with all your strength and with all your mind, and 'Love your neighbour as yourself." "You have answered correctly," Jesus replied. "Do this and you will live."[2] This is an immutable statement, always has been and always will be!

What is 'just'? A crib from a legal lexicon states: - *'It is that which accords with the perfect rights of others'*. By just is also understood full and perfect, such as a just weight." It is God's perfect right; it must be conceded in view of all that has been discussed, to decide that it is against His Law to violate agapé by disobedience and He is absolutely entitled to dispense justice as He sees fit. What is 'justice'? Justice is the appropriate redress, *under the law*, appropriate to the behaviour of an individual, whether said behaviour be considered good or bad by any individual. (My definition). So, hopefully, we have established another aspect of the character of God- He is just!

A retrospective visit to the Garden of Eden for a minute; He could not have expressed His agapé much more clearly positively than He did by placing them in the Garden of Eden, could He? They had it made! They had been made in His likeness so He knew exactly what opportunities there would be for them to exercise their free will so He used the KISS principle; - keep it simple son- and He made it as simple as He could with regard to them being able to remain in agapé with Him. In order to be obedient, it is, according to any system of reasoned argument, imperative that there is an opportunity to be disobedient. If you have no choice, you are not being obedient you are being manipulated and manipulation is not compatible with agapé. Our Father planted two particular trees, we know He planted them together because they were in the 'middle' of the garden and there is only one middle! In order for them to evidence their obedience they had only to obey the one simple command: - "You must not eat from the tree of the knowledge of good and evil."[3] Now we see with such amazing clarity the paradoxical nature of God, right next to the source of separation was the source of reconciliation, the tree of life!; His son, Jeshua, said "I am the way and the truth and the life. No one comes to the Father except through me,"[4] but at the time Jeshua was not available to man as a man: "And the Lord God said, "The man has now become like one of us, knowing good and evil. He must not be allowed to reach out his hand and take also from the tree of life and eat and live forever."[5] Later God made other provisions. Revelation states:- "Whoever has ears, let them hear what the Spirit says to the churches. To the one who is victorious, I will give the right to eat from the tree of life, which is in the paradise of God,"[6] right alongside what would prove to be the source of His wrath and vengeance, the tree of knowledge. "The Lord is a God who avenges. O God who avenges, shine forth."[7] "It is mine to avenge; I will repay. In due time their foot will slip; their day of disaster is near and their doom rushes upon them."[8] And He does not change! Note that in Eden they were barred from reaching out their hands to take from the tree but under the New Covenant He will give the right to eat. He demonstrates His mercy and compassion; He reveals His Fathers' heart. I propose to investigate this paradox further and to demonstrate its' validity. Moving on to the flood we learn from genesis 6 that 'sons of God' and Nephilim were on the earth. Were these one and the same is conjectural but what is evident is that they were not human. Again, using reasoned argument, we know this because they were attracted to the daughters of men, humans, mankind, man, humankind according to which translation you prefer; clearly, they were what we might term aliens. It occurs to me that it was the seductive nature of the women which was the root of the intercourses which produced the hybrid children referred to in verse 4. The basis of this observation is this:- "To the woman he said, "I will make your pains in childbearing very severe; with painful labour you will give birth to children. Your desire will be for your husband, and he will rule over you."[9] Sorry ladies, but it basically says the same in every translation. "The Nephilim were on the earth in those days and also afterward when the sons of God went to the daughters of humans and had children by them."[10] Is this why "The Lord regretted that he had made human beings on the earth, and his heart was deeply troubled."[11] Because "The Lord saw how great the wickedness of the human race had become on the earth, and that every inclination of the thoughts of the human heart was only evil all the time."[12] Eventually He made His decision:- "So the Lord said, "I will wipe from the face of the earth the human race I have created and with them the animals, the birds and the creatures that move along the ground for I regret that I have made them.[13]

That's it! He is saying I have had enough! "But Noah found favour in the eyes of the Lord."[14] This is where agapé kicks in! Still needing to be Himself (agapé) He decided to select a representative group from among the human race whom He would set apart and deal specifically with them in order to achieve His totally selfish end of what we now know to be to find a bride for His son. We are investigating the paradox so we should not be surprised at His dealings with Pharaoh and Egypt in the course of establishing His chosen people as a nation. In Exodus 33:19 God states His case unequivocally:- "And the Lord said, "I will cause all my goodness to pass in front of you, and I will proclaim my name, the Lord, in your presence. I will have mercy on whom I will have mercy, and I will have compassion on whom I will have compassion."[15] Now we have an even more amazing incidence of paradox because we also learn in Exodus that He entered into a covenant with His chosen people in spite (or maybe because of) of the fact that He knew that they were absolutely unreliable and inclined to infidelity, and that He was going to have to vent His wrath upon them! The Northern tribes were subjugated and dispersed throughout the nations; Ham and Judah were comprehensively violated and taken into exile in Babylon, but He anointed certain individuals who, through the auspices of the Holy Spirit, maintained His word and manifested His agapé in the interest of the redemption of man

So here we have the paradox; an all-powerful, selfish, wrathful, terrifying, and thoroughly, it appears, unpleasant God who is also agapé, merciful, compassionate, long-suffering and a thoroughly good chap. Yes! - the same person, not bipolar or schizophrenic but the *one* true God! If it is still an obstacle it will have to be faced and got round in some other way, if my efforts in 'circumnavigation' have been of no avail then you are stuck and can go no further. This coupled with the fact that He is unchanging demands that we put our Hellenistic mindset to death and adopt the mind of Christ- the Hebraic mindset which just accepts God just as He is without trying to make sense of the unfathomable. His unfathomability (I just had to get that in, I think I invented it, it's not in the dictionary or thesaurus!) has already been established; let us look at another of His characteristics which has not been seriously investigated yet, His propensity for vengeance. Vengeance, as just about always translated from original texts, means exactly what it says on the can. 'Infliction of injury, harm, humiliation or the like, on a person or persons by another who has been harmed by that or those persons(s) i.e., violent revenge.' (Dictionary definition). There is no arguing about it, this trait was made absolutely clear right away in Deuteronomy:- "It is mine to avenge; I will repay. In due time their foot will slip; their day of disaster is near and their doom rushes upon them."[16] "See now that I myself am he! There is no God besides me. I put to death, and I bring to life, I have wounded, and I will heal, and no one can deliver out of my hand. I lift my hand to heaven and solemnly swear: As surely as I live forever, when I sharpen my flashing sword and my hand grasps it in judgement, I will take vengeance on my adversaries and repay those who hate me."[17] This is why Jeshua told us to love our enemies:- "But to you who are listening I say: Love your enemies, do good to those who hate you."[18] Vengeance belongs to God! Turning the other cheek and welcoming home the prodigal son is recognition of this fact

Of course, I know that the comfortable and naive will not appreciate the whole truth and there are mutterings about 'unbalance', but this is the whole point of the messages I have been given and am passing on. God has stated that He is sick of a sick church; we have had prophesy after prophesy that we were headed for, and are now experiencing, a major shake-up; part of that sickness is the false teaching of unlimited grace and the lack of good teaching which reveals the *whole* nature of God. This, under the anointing of the Holy Spirit, brings conviction, conviction leads to either rejection or repentance, and repentance to salvation This is why Jeshua told us to make Disciples not followers: - "Therefore go and make disciples of all nations, baptizing them in the name of the Father and of the Son and of the Holy Spirit, and teaching them to obey everything I have commanded you, and surely I am with you always, to the very end of the age." He said[19] Read the small print at the bottom again: - *"and teaching them to obey everything I have commanded you."* He also said, "In the same way, those of you who do not give up everything you have cannot be my disciples."[20]

When do we hear of this teaching? Partly because it is not palatable and tasty and partly because true preaching (exhortation, teaching, prophesy, truth-saying) can only be shared from an individuals' own testimony under the anointing of the Holy Spirit; you cannot learn it, if you think you can then you are just an orator, maybe a very good one but just an orator, nevertheless. An orator is a person who takes 500 words to say what an anointed person can say in 50 (my definition). Read Acts 10:34ff in 10 verses, fewer than 100 words, the Gospel was preached, the Holy Spirit fell and the baptism of those who had heard was arranged. The same thing had happened in Acts 8 34ff when Philip met the Ethiopian eunuch. The sickness in the church is the result of people only listening to what their itching ears want to hear: - "For the time will come when people will not put up with sound doctrine. Instead, to suit their own desires, they will gather around them a great number of teachers to say what their itching ears want to hear."[21] All of Paul's letters were his testimony of his own walk with God and evidenced in his knowledge of the scriptures; the Tanakh. I have no problem emphasising that part of the gospel which so many avoid through fear and self-interest because I carry a burden for those who Jeshua was referring to as recorded by Matthew: - "Not everyone who says to me, 'Lord, Lord,' will enter the kingdom of heaven, but only the one who does the will of my Father who is in heaven. Many will say to me on that day, 'Lord, Lord, did we not prophesy in your name and in your name drive out demons and, in your name, perform many miracles?' Then I will tell them plainly, 'I never knew you. Away from me you evildoers!'"[22]

God's wrath and His judgement are coming, make no mistake about it, where there is absolutely no fear, awe or reverence now, there soon will be! We shall all bow before Him with fear and trembling but those of us who know of His love and have met His conditions (nearly all of His promises are conditional.) Bible study, as opposed to bible commentary, might be 'profitable for teaching, rebuking, correcting, and training in righteousness,' for disciples, we are safe in Christ. Are you? Read Matthew 7 again then check out your standing and eligibility as a disciple. Time for another breather, it has been a while since the last bit of the climb was taken on; I think the gap was needed for the experience of that part of the climb to be assimilated and digested. The words 'left to stew' have come to mind a number of times. I think the next part of the climb will involve an insight into Father's 'resolve' and some examples of His grace and mercy in action.

CHAPTER 8

MORE REALLY HARD STUFF - TRUTH, AND NOTHING BUT!

This is going to be a quite exciting part of the climb as we review the paradox in action and investigate what He has revealed about the early stages of His plan for redemption. We now know, I hope, that His directive and utterly selfish will is to provide a bride for His son. We are not saved for our benefit but for His; salvation is not a reward for having made a decision or doing the right thing, it is because we are part of the plan He has for the fulfilment of His will. Jeshua said; "No one can come to me unless the Father who sent me draws them, and I will raise them up at the last day."[1] And Paul addresses Titus thus; - "Paul, a servant of God and an apostle of Jesus Christ to further the faith of *God's elect and their knowledge of the truth that leads to godliness.*"[2] There are many more scriptures testifying to the fact that it is Gods directive will that His bride will be there for His Son. Jeshua also said:-"For many are invited, but few are chosen."[3] This was spoken at the end of the parable about those who went to the wedding feast improperly dressed, do you think these might be the same to whom He was referring in Matthew; "Not everyone who says to me, 'Lord, Lord,' will enter the kingdom of heaven, but only the one who does the will of my Father who is in heaven. Many will say to me on that day, 'Lord, Lord, did we not prophesy in your name and in your name drive out demons and, in your name, perform many miracles?' Then I will tell them plainly, 'I never knew you. Away from me you evildoers!'"[4]?

How can we be sure of our election? Easy, by fulfilling the conditions laid down by our Father; "For it is not those who hear the law who are righteous in God's sight, but it is those who obey the law who will be declared righteous."[5] And the law is, according to Jeshua:- "Love the Lord your God with all your heart and with all your soul and with all your strength and with all your mind'; and, 'Love your neighbour as yourself."[6] N.B. This applies to spouses and siblings! God sees every act! Enough preamble, now we will start up the 'not-too-steep' slope of discovery of the origins of His plans for the elect, His chosen people. We have already established the evidence of His fury and vengeance on an utterly corrupted world in the account of the flood. We have also established the evidence of His perseverance and grace in His dealings with Noah; I repeat some verses from Genesis 6:- "The Lord saw how great the wickedness of the human race had become on the earth, and that every inclination of the thoughts of the human heart was only evil all the time. The Lord regretted that he had made human beings on the earth, and his heart was deeply troubled. But Noah found favour in the eyes of the Lord" (verses 5ff). Why did Noah find favour? Yes, God considered him to be a righteous man, but God also chose him to continue the human race in order to fulfil *His* purposes. One of my favourite quotes:- "In Him we were also chosen, having been predestined according to the plan of him who works out everything in conformity with the purpose of his will."[7]

So, to cut a long story short, Noah and his family re-populated the earth. But by the time of Abram's generation, they were back to square one, Godless idolators bent on accessing the heavens so great was their vanity; Babylon (confusion) had arrived with the result that God wrought confusion upon them and scattered them throughout the earth. But here we go again:- "So also Abraham believed God, and it was credited to him as righteousness."[8] Let us consider Noah and Abram further. "This is the account of Noah and his family. Noah was a righteous man, blameless among the people of his time, and he walked faithfully with God."[9] There is no evidence that Abram was of the same ilk, he was a citizen of Ur of the Chaldees. Ur, according to those who ought to know, is derived from the phrase in the ancient languages to mean 'the abode of Nanna', Nanna was the god of the moon in ancient Assyrian and Babylonian mythology. So, it would appear that Noah was chosen for his potential to re-populate the earth with Godly people which did not work out; and Abram was randomly chosen from amidst a Godless, idolatrous, and decadent civilisation to effect God's approbative will anyway. What both men had in common was that they heard God speak to them loud and clear! Noah, we know, walked with God so it might be assumed that he was familiar with the 'art' (for want of a better word) of discoursing with God or at least an experienced listener to His words.

Not so with Abram it would appear, all we are told is that:- "The Lord had said to Abram, "Go from your country, your people and your father's household to the land I will show you. "I will make you into a great nation, and I will bless you; I will make your name great, and you will be a blessing. I will bless those who bless you, and whoever curses you I will curse; and all peoples on earth will be blessed through you."[10] What is wonderfully clear is that:- "Faith comes from hearing the message, and the message is heard through the word of/ about Christ/God."[11] depending on your choice of translation. The whole truth is not bound by the context; the whole truth is that when God speaks to an individual, whether it be about personal salvation or not, His words will bring conviction and that conviction will incur faith and that faith will incur action. There are the occasional exceptions, as discussed earlier, with regard to the exceptionally stubborn and hard-hearted, but, by and large, the statement is valid. We know why God chose Abram, not because he had any particular virtue in his original condition but because he would be obedient and eventually bring about the fruition of God's perfect plan to find a bride for His Son. He was going to make him into a great nation from which would come not only redemption for a portion of the human race but also a bride for the redeemer. Abram was told to do nothing initially except:- "Go from your country, your people and your father's household to the land I will show you."[12] He was likely quite comfortable in his 'civilised', 'cultured', cosy world but he was just told to come out of it. He did, not knowing where he was going, but was looking for a city with foundations whose architect and builder is God. (Cf: Hebrews 11:8-11).

Doesn't all this sound familiar? Are we who are called not asked to leave everything, come out of the world, and trust God with regard as to where we will have to go? Abraham, as he later become known, is the father of all believers:- "Therefore, the promise comes by faith, so that it may be by grace and may be guaranteed to all Abraham's offspring, not only to those who are of the law but also to those who have the faith of Abraham. He is the father of us all."[13] This is very significant because it reveals that salvation comes through birth and birth alone; Jeshua said, "Very truly I tell you, no one can see the kingdom of God unless they are born again."[14] Not by preaching, indoctrination or persuasion but only by birth, by coming out of the world leaving it behind and trusting God for your future, by putting the old self to death and taking the first steps of faith. Faith says Paul "is confidence in what we hope for and assurance about what we do not see."[15]

We have seen that Abram was called out from Ur of the Chaldees, Ur was representative of the nations which had been judged and dealt with by God following the tower of Babel incident; they had all been rejected by God because they had caused Him great offence, this needs to be borne in mind as we head further up the mountain. God had rejected the whole of humanity except Abram whom he had chosen to father a select people, a people set apart, who *He* would call His own and who *He* would establish in His own special land which *He* would also call His own. This is the pattern which God has selected, to choose men and women who have no virtue of their own, no Godliness, no righteousness, no upright moral character, nothing of themselves to commend them but to talk them into leaving Ur behind them and to follow Him in total obedience and faith. This pattern can be recognised throughout the scriptures. The whole point is that we are like Abram, and we are no different than anyone else except that we have been chosen even before the creation to be children of Abraham, children of the Living God. "For he chose us in him before the creation of the world to be holy and blameless in his sight."[16] "Remember the wonders he has done, his miracles, and the judgements he pronounced, you his servants, the descendants of Israel, his chosen ones, the children of Jacob"[17]. "But you are a chosen people, a royal priesthood, a holy nation, God's special possession, that you may declare the praises of him who called you out of darkness into his wonderful light."[18]. If you are a Gentile remember that you have been grafted into Israel; Paul addressed the (Gentile) Romans thus:- "If some of the branches have been broken off, and you, though a wild olive shoot, have been grafted in among the others and now share in the nourishing sap from the olive root, do not consider yourself to be superior to those other branches. If you do, consider this: You do not support the root, but the root supports you". You will say then, "Branches were broken off so that I could be grafted in."[19]

An interesting facet of Abram's character comes to light, his fallibility; in verse 1 he had been told to leave his father's household, but Abram took his dad, Terah, with him. Now we know that Terah was an idolator; "Joshua said to all the people, "This is what the Lord, the God of Israel, says: 'Long ago your ancestors, including Terah the father of Abraham and Nahor, lived beyond the Euphrates River and worshiped other gods."[20] 'Terah', according to most sources means 'wild goat', 'delay', 'loiter', 'wanderer'; it seems likely that this misdemeanour, or whatever one cares to call it, accounts for the fact that they only got as far as Haran when their journey came to a halt; and they sojourned in Haran until Terah died. After this Abram was inclined to resume his journey to Canaan. We do not know exactly when or how it was revealed that Canaan was the destination which had been determined, perhaps Terah had been instrumental in the decision making, but we do know that by the time they had left Ur, Canaan had become their destination: (Cf: Genesis 11:31). Note that Abram was seventy-five when he left Haran so I guess his paternal prospects were not too rosy; it must have caused him some consternation when, having arrived at Shechem in Canaan, God told him that it would be his offspring to whom He would give this land and we are told he built an altar there, an altar is a place of slaughter or sacrifice. There is much speculation about Abram's altars, but we can be sure that the offerings made were burnt offerings as the Law demanding 'sin' offerings had not been given; what the significance of this altar and the offering made on it is between Abram and his God. God works on a 'need to know' basis with me: if I need to know He will tell me otherwise I mind my own business, [another piece of wise counsel- no fee:-] Any man who sticks his nose into God's business uninvited is a fool indeed! This is only the second altar, so far as we know, to be built, the first had been built by Noah on leaving the ark for dry land so they are highly significant with regard to the progress towards man's redemption. "From there he went on toward the hills east of Bethel and pitched his tent, with Bethel on the west and Ai on the east. There he built an altar to the Lord and called on the name of the Lord."[21]

This is very significant and illuminating because 'Bethel' means 'house of God' and 'Ai' means 'place of ruin or ruins'; note that Abram's tent was pitched between the two so when he faced the House of God his back was towards the ruins! He built another altar there and then headed off towards the Negev and thence to Egypt. Abram's fallibility is demonstrated again during his visit to Egypt, when he resorted to lies and deceit with regard to his wife, Sarai: (Genesis 12:10ff). Because of this Abram acquired wealth but at the cost to Pharaoh and his household of the suffering of serious diseases. Thence back to that place between Bethel and Ai where he had built his altar and he 'called on the name of the Lord'. The incident in Egypt reveals the paradoxical nature of our God again and establishes the pattern of His dealings with humanity.

Before going further, I will remind you again that God does not change, if you have not come to terms with this truth then you cannot go further up the mountain! The nations in scripture denote the idolatrous and the ungodly, they have no virtue in God's eyes and are subject to His wrath and judgement, this is implicit throughout the whole of scripture. The only exception is Israel which had not been established yet but was part of God's plan as revealed to Abram. We see God's dealing with the nation of Egypt for the benefit of Israel in this incident and this fact must be accepted, there is no other explanation. This fact will be evidenced time and time again throughout the rest of history and will be evidenced again in the near future. This is the first time that God had made His intentions clear, it must have been extraordinarily difficult for Abram to grasp; it is not difficult to understand the reality of personal salvation, to know that we have been chosen and bought at great cost, but to understand the working of almighty God, His ultimate purpose and the means by which He will "work out everything in conformity with the purpose of his will." (Ephesians 1:11 again) is beyond the mind of the majority of mankind as has already been established.

It is likely that we shall continue up the mountain in the company of Abram and his descendants for a while hoping that our paradoxical Father is going to reveal more of Himself to us as we climb.

CHAPTER 9

FATHER ABRAHAM - REGARDING COVENANTS AND CONDITIONS

It was stated during the last part of the climb that the nations in scripture denote the idolatrous and the ungodly, they have no virtue in God's eyes and are subject to His wrath and judgement, this is implicit throughout the whole of scripture. It seems prudent to go off on a tangential path at this time rather than straight up. Since we are going to be faced with the facts of His dealing with the nations; let us follow the path of the nations, we learn that: - "These are the clans of Noah's sons, according to their lines of descent, within their nations. From these the nations spread out over the earth after the flood."[1] "The sons of Noah were Shem, Ham and Japheth."[2] Following a drunken episode which involved Ham seeing his father's nakedness[3] "Noah awoke from his wine and found out what his youngest son had done to him, he said, "Cursed be Canaan! The lowest of slaves will he be to his brothers." He also said, "Praise be to the Lord, the God of Shem! May Canaan be the slave of Shem. May God extend Japheth's territory; may Japheth live in the tents of Shem, and may Canaan be the slave of Japheth."[4] The descendants of Japheth spread out into relative insignificance, not so in the cases of Ham and Shem; one of Ham's descendants was Nimrod. The first centres of his kingdom were Babylon, Uruk, Akkad and Kalneh, in Shinar.[5] Among his other kin were Egypt or Mizraim who was the forefather of a number of tribes, among whom were the Philistines.

Canaan was also the forefather of a number of tribes. Later the Canaanite clans scattered, and the borders of Canaan reached from Sidon toward Gerar as far as Gaza, and then toward Sodom, Gomorrah, Admah and Zeboyim, as far as Lasha.[6] Now let us move on to Babylon which had been established, as we have seen, by Nimrod, one of Ham's descendants and again review the consequences of the behaviour of the descendants of Ham: "The Lord said, "If as one people speaking the same language they have begun to do this, then nothing they plan to do will be impossible for them. Come, let us go down and confuse their language so they will not understand each other. "So, the Lord scattered them from there over all the earth, and they stopped building the city."[7] Although it has not been revealed to us exactly what the offence against Noah was, or why God chose to curse Canaan rather than his father and also to confer on Shem such ascendance over Canaan, we can follow the thread of God's perfect plan.

Canaan became an anathema God.[8,9] Its inhabitants had resorted to all sorts of abominations including the worship of demonic idols and false gods, child sacrifices, incest, homosexuality, and temple prostitution. God's plan had two major objectives; first to destroy a culture which had become an anathema to Him and, secondly to fulfil His promises made to Abraham[10] and later to Jacob.[11] In fact it was made clear to the Israelites on their way towards the 'promised land' that it was not because of any virtues that they might consider themselves to have, because He calls them 'a stiff-necked people'[12] Rather, His prime objective was to wreak His judgement upon them! "After the Lord your God has driven them out before you, do not say to yourself, "The Lord has brought me here to take possession of this land because of my righteousness." No, it is on account of the wickedness of these nations that the Lord is going to drive them out before you. It is not because of your righteousness or your integrity that you are going in to take possession of their land; but on account of the wickedness of these nations, the Lord your God will drive them out before you, to accomplish what he swore to your fathers, to Abraham, Isaac and Jacob."[13] "The fierce anger of the Lord will not turn back until he fully accomplishes the purposes of his heart. In days to come you will understand this"[14] I think, remembering the intractable fact that God does not change, that it might be appropriate in these dark days to read the first chapter of Paul's letter to the Romans.

Returning to Shem, who had not gazed upon his father's nakedness; he lived to become the founder of a great dynasty who became known as the Semites, from whom came the Israelites and the Jews. At the time of the incident involving Noah's nakedness Shem's brother Japheth had also averted his gaze and avoided the curse of his father, in fact Noah had ordained that Japheth should enjoy the benefits of Shem's kinship.[15] Twelve generations later Abram was born, interestingly, this branch of the clan had gone the way of the rest and inhabited the area which included Ur as has already been discussed. As we go on now, we shall see the prophesies which God had given to Noah come to fruition. Following their departure from Egypt and their nomadic lifestyle (Cf: Genesis 13:) they arrived at a situation which, due to their prosperity (the grace of God in action) it became necessary to part company. Lot, having been given the choice by his gracious uncle, chose the rich plains of Jordan, Abram lived in Canaan while Lot pitched his tents near Sodom. (Are pennies starting to drop?) Abram pitched his tents near Mamre, among allies, where he built another altar to the Lord. Chapter 14 of Genesis is powerfully rich and warrants a great deal of study, so I am going to try and establish just a few footholds to help us on our upward path.

First a quick glance at the four kings who went to war against the rebellious kings who ruled the area in which Lot had chosen to reside. Amraphel was a Babylonian, he was of Shinar (Nimrod), Arioch is of Ellasar also Babylonian; Kedorlaomer probably means 'servant of Lagamaru 'an Elamite deity. Elamite is considered by the linguists as a 'language isolate' which means that it has no related languages and is consequently very difficult to study and interpret. Does this remind you of Babylon? The last king, Tidal, is most interesting, he is reported as being of Goiim or Goyim, which in Hebrew means 'nation' or, more particularly 'non-Jew'! It seems that in the ensuing battle God's judgement against Sodom and Gomorrah was already evident, they drew up their battle lines in a position which greatly favoured their enemy- the Valley of Siddim. In the ensuing rout Lot and company were carried off along with everything else. Now Abram had chosen to reside at Mamre among allies and, having been informed of Lot's distress he set off with 318 of his own men and possibly with support from his allies- we do not know, he overtook and routed the four kings, recovered all the loot and booty, and returned to Canaan. We are told that the king of Sodom came out to meet him, and so did someone else! "Then Melchizedek king of Salem brought out bread and wine. He was priest of God Most High."[16] Melchizedek is mentioned only once again before Paul's letter to the Hebrews and that is in Psalm 110 verse 4 where Yeshua is stated as being a priest in the order of Melchizedek; Paul states "First, the name Melchizedek means 'king of righteousness'; then also, 'king of Salem' means king of peace. Without father or mother, without genealogy, without beginning of days or end of life, resembling the Son of God, he remains a priest forever."[17] This about sums up our revelation of who Melchizedek might be; there is no point in speculation but what is clear is that God is establishing this priesthood as the ultimate priesthood, it precedes the Levites and establishes Yeshua's status in the greater order of things. He was not a priest of the order of Levi but of the order of Melchizedek. "If perfection could have been attained through the Levitical priesthood, and indeed the law given to the people established that priesthood, why was there still need for another priest to come, one in the order of Melchizedek, not in the order of Aaron?"[18]

Returning to Abram, we are given more insight into his character at the end of chapter 14: "The king of Sodom said to Abram, "Give me the people and keep the goods for yourself." But Abram said to the king of Sodom, "With raised hand I have sworn an oath to the Lord, God Most High, Creator of heaven and earth, that I will accept nothing belonging to you, not even a thread or the strap of a sandal, so that you will never be able to say, 'I made Abram rich."[19] Before resuming the upward path it might be appropriate to consider some other aspects of the content of Genesis 14. So far as Abram is concerned, we have been made aware of his fallibility, he left his inheritance for Egypt, albeit for sound 'natural' reasons, and resorted to lies and deceit while he was there; having returned he exhibited his grace nature in giving Lot the choice. Lot suffered the consequences of his selfish nature, but Abram again showed grace and compassion by going to his rescue; and Abram showed that his relationship with his God was maturing to the extent that he would not want the pagans to be credited with his prosperity this time! We are also being given some insight as to how God deals with the nations as opposed to Israel. Notice that, in spite of Abram's fallibility God stays with him, whereas He uses the nations, especially here, Egypt and Babylon and the nations (Goiim), to deal with Israel; this pattern will be epitomised later in His dealing with the northern tribes and Judah at the hands of Assyria and Babylon. The ultimate priesthood from which the Messiah will come is revealed and God's faithfulness towards Abram is revealed in spite of his shortcomings.

"After this, the word of the Lord came to Abram in a vision: "Do not be afraid, Abram. I am your shield, your very great reward." or in other translations "I will protect you, and your reward will be great."[20] The latter seems likely since Abram's response was "Sovereign Lord, what can you give me since I remain childless and the one who will inherit my estate is Eliezer of Damascus?" And Abram said, "You have given me no children; so a servant in my household will be my heir."[21] Then the word of the Lord came to him: "This man will not be your heir, but a son who is your own flesh and blood will be your heir." He took him outside and said, "Look up at the sky and count the stars if indeed you can count them." Then he said to him, "So shall your offspring be." Abram believed the Lord, and he credited it to him as righteousness."[22] So here is doubting, unsure, wayward, fallible, Abram remonstrating with God until he decides to actually believe Him, then his belief is credited to him as righteousness. Does all this sound familiar? Then, would you believe it? he kicks off again! "He also said to him, "I am the Lord, who brought you out of Ur of the Chaldeans to give you this land to take possession of it." But Abram said, "Sovereign Lord, how can I know that

I will gain possession of it?"[23] Now we see the wonderful grace of God manifest in His response to Abram's question; here He is establishing the pattern by which we can understand His dealings with His chosen people as opposed to the nations. "So, the Lord said to him, "Bring me a heifer, a goat and a ram, each three years old, along with a dove and a young pigeon." Abram brought all these to him, cut them in two and arranged the halves opposite each other; the birds, however, he did not cut in half. Then birds of prey came down on the carcasses, but Abram drove them away."[24]

This is the first recorded blood covenant; another pattern being established; this is God's answer to Abram's question- a covenant. A covenant is absolutely binding, it is widely understood that the significance of the two covenanters walking between the two halves of the slain animal is that should either of them break the covenant that they should suffer the same fate. It is vital that the sacrifice and the shedding of blood is not defiled in any way by duplicitous thoughts or intentions, no unspoken 'get out' clauses are incorporated into it; it is absolutely inviolable and sacrosanct. That is why Abram drove away the birds of prey- scavengers and violators who would have defiled the covenant. So, Abram's question is answered with a covenant, note that this is a less usual form of covenant in that it is unilateral and unconditional; God made the terms of this covenant to apply only to Himself, it did not require anything on the part of Abram, so it was unconditional. Compare Leviticus 26:3/4:-"*If* you follow my decrees and are careful to obey my commands, I will send you rain in its season, and the ground will yield its crops and the trees their fruit." or John 15:10:-"*If* you keep my commands, you will remain in my love, just as I have kept my Father's commands and remain in his love." These are bilateral and conditional covenants; the promise is honoured by the One covenanter (God) *if* the conditions are met by the other covenanter (us). This is grossly overlooked by so many who mistakenly think that all of God's promises are there to be partaken of at no cost, that unlimited and inviolable grace are there to be taken as an entitlement? "As the sun was setting, Abram fell into a deep sleep, and a thick and dreadful darkness came over him. Then the Lord said to him, "Know for certain that for four hundred years your descendants will be strangers in a country not their own and that they will be enslaved and mistreated there. But I will punish the nation they serve as slaves, and afterward they will come out with great possessions."[25]

Was it grace that required of God that Abram be, for want of a better word, 'anaesthetized'? Would it have been too much for the elderly man to bear? To know, in his fully cognitive state, what God had in mind for his descendants. Abram's descendants, we know, we are not, generally speaking, as obedient and compliant as even Abram and he didn't exactly present himself as the clay in the potters' hands, did he? His descendants would exhibit all the lumps, stones, grit, and debris which are the despair of the potter, and God would deal with them as He saw fit! Abram, however, was given the prophesy as gently as possible, maybe the Father-God wanted him to be aware of the true cost and trials of fatherhood, who knows? To move on "You, however, will go to your ancestors in peace and be buried at a good old age. In the fourth generation your descendants will come back here, for the sin of the Amorites (one of the clans of Canaan) has not yet reached its full measure."[26] Here we see God's directive will in action; we know that "In him we were also chosen, having been predestined according to the plan of him who works out everything in conformity with the purpose of his will,"[27] God had pre-ordained the destiny of Abram, of his descendants and of the nations who were currently inhabiting the promised land. Interestingly He decided to spare Abram the trials that would face his descendants and grant him peace and old age, the Amorites who had been Abram's allies, however, were destined to go the way of the nations as their sin would increase until they were ripe, in God's eyes, to be evicted from Canaan in preparation for the establishment of Israel.

It was custom for a covenant to become binding when the two parties walked between the halves of the severed beast, variously there were other activities incorporated into the ritual, but the joint passage of the covenanters was a fundamental requirement. In the case of a unilateral, unconditional covenant such as this there would be no cause for the passive party to make this passage, but we do see that God still played His part when the Shechinah, or majesty of God passed between the pieces. "When the sun had set and darkness had fallen, a smoking fire pot with a blazing torch appeared and passed between the pieces. On that day the Lord made a covenant with Abram and said, "To your descendants I give this land, from the Wadi of Egypt to the great river, the Euphrates-- the land of the Kenites, Kenizzites, Kadmonites, Hittites, Perizzites, Rephaites, Amorites, Canaanites, Girgashites and Jebusites."[28] Even after all this dear old Abram still could not get it right! Sarai, his wife, dropped him in it and he went for it hook, line and sinker. "She said to Abram, "The Lord has kept me from having children. Go, sleep with my slave; perhaps I can build a family through her." Abram agreed to what Sarai said."[29] Just consider the consequences of his folly:- "He slept with Hagar, and she conceived. When she knew she was pregnant, she began to despise her mistress. Then Sarai said to Abram, "You are responsible for the wrong I am suffering. I put my slave in your arms, and now that she knows she is pregnant, she despises me. May the Lord judge between you and me." "Your slave is in your hands," Abram said. "Do with her whatever you think best." Then Sarai mistreated Hagar; so she fled from her. The angel of the Lord found Hagar near a spring in the desert; it was the spring that is beside the road to Shur. And he said, "Hagar, slave of Sarai, where have you come from, and where are you going?" "I'm running away from my mistress Sarai," she answered. Then the angel of the Lord told her, "Go back to your mistress and submit to her."[30] We are seeing the fruits of questionable, fleshy, impatient, and foolhardy behaviour; in spite of all God's dealings and communications with Abram, he blew it again; the result- Ishmael! Abram chose to have intercourse with Hagar who was out of Egypt, one of the idolatrous nations, and was on her way back there but by the grace of God was waylaid by an angel sent to assure Hagar her cries had been heard and answered by a merciful God.[31]

In spite of having prophesied against the nations, God has made clear His intent to appoint the descendants of one man, in spite of all his shortcomings and foibles, to father a select people who would be set aside to fulfil His purposes; who would establish a unique nation and who would, for all intents and purposes, behave no differently from the nations from which they had been taken out but would remain special to the Father, to whom He would remain faithful and from whom He would choose His Son's bride. So much more could be discovered on this phase of the climb but, for now, we leave Abram and Sarai. The next phase will involve Abraham (father of many) being changed along with his name.

CHAPTER 10

TIME TO TARRY AWHILE? -
OF GRACE AND FAVOUR

Having spent some time in the company of Abram and not really having made a lot of upward progress with regard to our inquiry into the paradoxical nature of our God, I have had to consider whether it might be constructive to spend a bit more time with him (Abram) before resuming the vertical ascent. This far up the mountain one's efforts at upward progress are curtailed by mists, snowstorms, hidden gullies, icy terrain and the like. Such encounters render it prudent to slow the pace a little or take a less demanding route, so I have decided to tarry awhile and continue on the more accessible way for the time being with Abram, shortly to become Abraham. Let us consider Abrams walk with God so far; he has proven to be, in spite of his established personal relationship with God; erratic, impatient, faithless, self, (rather than God) motivated, and, on the whole, unreliable. We left Abram at the end of Genesis chapter 16 following the birth of Ishmael. Ishmael, according to Genesis 17:20, was made a father of nations but then withered into obscurity whereas Isaac, who had not even been born yet, was the one with whom God would make his covenant.[1]

In spite of all Abram's faults, "When Abram was ninety-nine years old, the Lord appeared to him and said, "I am God Almighty; walk before me faithfully and be blameless. Then I will make my covenant between me and you and will greatly increase your numbers."[2] Here is the most remarkable act of grace to be witnessed; even before Christ walked the earth we have a case of an ordinary sinner, just like any of us, being redeemed, born again, and chosen to fulfil God's purposes for His glory. A sovereign act of grace and mercy granted towards an individual with no redeeming features of his own with the sole intent, on God's part, that this individual will bring about the fulfilment of His impeccable plan. "Abram fell face down, and God said to him, No longer will you be called Abram; your name will be Abraham, for I have made you a father of many nations. I will make you very fruitful; I will make nations of you, and kings will come from you. I will establish my covenant as an everlasting covenant between me and you and your descendants after you for the generations to come, to be your God and the God of your descendants after you. The whole land of Canaan, where you now reside as a foreigner, I will give as an everlasting possession to you and your descendants after you; and I will be their God. Then God said to Abraham, As for you, you must keep my covenant, you, and your descendants after you for the generations to come. This is my covenant with you and your descendants after you, the covenant you are to keep. Every male among you shall be circumcised. You are to undergo circumcision, and it will be the sign of the covenant between me and you."[3] Abraham fell facedown; he laughed and said to himself, "Will a son be born to a man a hundred years old? Will Sarah bear a child at the age of ninety?"[4]

This is the second time in chapter 17 that it is recorded that Abraham 'fell face down', there are 20 occurrences of this term being used in the scriptures and two of them are in relation to Abraham in Genesis 17. It occurs to me that if God is having that much of an impact on an individual it is right and proper, if not involuntary, to fall prostrate before Him, literally! Having experienced the awesome intensity and glory of God, the overwhelming power of His presence, how could one remain standing? Is not the most profound act of worship to fall prostrate before Him, speechless in His presence; just to be still on one's face and know that He is God? Yes, there are lots of harps, tambourines, cymbals, lyres, stringed instruments and the like recommended for the purpose of praising God but "Yet a time is coming and has now come when the true worshippers will worship the Father in the Spirit and in truth, for they are the kind of worshippers the Father seeks."[5] This is a fact, praise is not synonymous with worship. Contrary to much popular misconception worship has no relationship with wattage, worship has to do with attitude; one antonym for attitude is 'position', the prone position is a good one! It is one thing to praise someone, quite another to worship them. It is one thing to accept Jesus as your Saviour but a totally different matter to make Him your Lord. To be flippant and presumptuous, to assume or imply that one term incorporates the other, in either case, is very dangerous! I quote Jeshua again "Not everyone who says to me, 'Lord, Lord,' will enter the kingdom of heaven, but only the one who does the will of my Father who is in heaven."[6] In one of my quiet times with the Lord when something someone had said inspired me to seek Father's opinion on the whole issue of praise and worship, He told me that praise and worship are not what you do, but are a condition of the soul!

Abraham fell facedown; he laughed and said to himself, "Will a son be born to a man a hundred years old? Will Sarah bear a child at the age of ninety?" I had to repeat this passage it is so poignant; we are witnessing this man enduring the 'born again' experience. Abraham and Sarai, both have had their names changed, after all they are now new creations! To all intents and purposes, they are both dead! Abraham had taken hold of God's promises, grasped them, tried to fulfil them through his own fleshy efforts, and finally sat down and conceded the fact that he was absolutely unable to fulfil anything of his own volition. Does his ring any bells? Having got to the stage where, so far as he was concerned, there was no chance of fathering a fulfilment of God's promise, he gave in! Now God moved! Then God said:- "Yes, but your wife Sarah will bear you a son, and you will call him Isaac. I will establish my covenant with him as an everlasting covenant for his descendants after him."[7] He had already told Abram that his name was to be changed to be 'Father of Many', father of nations and kings, that His covenant was to be valid for Abraham *and* his descendants after him; and that the whole land of Canaan was given as an everlasting possession to him and his descendants.

But there had been conditions!" A 'conditional' covenant. Then God said to Abraham, "As for you, you must keep my covenant, you, and your descendants after you for the generations to come. This is my covenant with you and your descendants after you, the covenant you are to keep. Every male among you shall be circumcised. You are to undergo circumcision, and it will be the sign of the covenant between me and you."[8]

What many 'born again' Christians do not realise is that many of God's promises are conditional! Let us start at the beginning, or at least fairly close to it, "*If* you follow my decrees and are careful to obey my commands, I will send you rain in its season, and the ground will yield its crops and the trees their fruit."[9] "So if you faithfully obey the commands I am giving you today, to love the Lord your God and to serve him with all your heart and with all your soul, then I will send rain on your land in its season; both autumn and spring rains, so that you may gather in your grain, new wine and olive oil"[10] "*If* you do whatever I command you and walk in obedience to me and do what is right in my eyes by obeying my decrees and commands, as David my servant did, I will be with you. I will build you a dynasty as enduring as the one I built for David and will give Israel to you."[10] "But, *if* you return to me and obey my commands, then even if your exiled people are at the farthest horizon, I will gather them from there and bring them to the place I have chosen as a dwelling for my Name."[11] And in the words of Jeshua:- "You are my friends *if* you do what I command, I no longer call you servants, because a servant does not know his master's business. Instead, I have called you friends, for everything that I learned from my Father I have made known to you."[12] All conditional, and there are many more! All teachings on unlimited grace and unconditional salvation are *false*, and totally contrary to scripture. I re-iterate; God does not change!

The scriptures themselves tell us that it is *all* relevant, we are not to add or delete any of it! We are going to leave Abraham shortly and resume our upward trek in pursuit of a greater understanding of our infallible, paradoxical, and unfathomable

God. In view of the current climate, both meteorological and political, I have to go back to basics, to truths that were discussed on the lower reaches of the mountain. We (humanity) are part of God's creation; even the most fervent atheistic so called 'scientists' have now had to concede the fact of creation, they may call it the 'big bang' but whatever you call it, it was an act of creation! Labels are meaningless, I shall discuss this further shortly. God is love,[13] and love must be an act of freewill, especially 'agapé' which is God's absolute and unique love. If one does not have freewill then one is incapable of agapé love; therefore, we were created with the faculty of freewill. In our fallen state, (the consequence of our ancestors exercising their freewill unwisely), we are all self-centred, never totally satisfied with what we have got, whatever it may be. Mankind's inclination without Christ, is to lust after more; more wealth, more power, more 'security', more food, more sex, more, more, more and more; but never more, in the case of the majority, of agapé love! The consequence of this condition is that most of mankind are going to 'look after number one' if necessary, at the expense of anyone lower in the ordinal sequence, this is a fact and the root of all conflicts.

The trouble with labels is that they generally do not do what is says on the tin, or the label. Take the label 'motor vehicle' what does it tell you? Hardly anything except that it probably involves wheels and an engine but even then, there might be exceptions; could be a car or a bus or a tank or a giant earth mover or an electrically propelled cycle. Most people, I guess, would assume that the 'motor vehicle' referred to would be a car, a van, a lorry, or a bus; one of the more usual or common types of motor vehicle; but in all likelihood they are wrong. Having a label, whether one appropriated by oneself for convenience, or having one thrust upon one by a third party with no intrinsic right to do so is a recipe for confusion, unreliability, blunder, deception, and conflict. Generic labels are the most insidious and malicious, not by intent but by misadventure (for want of a better word); Moslem, Jew, Christian, Asian, American, Chinese, communist, radical, athlete, banker, politician; I could go on and on. All generic labels, all terms which fail to enlighten anyone with regard to any individual who is categorised under the constraints of one of these assumed definitions. The label does not define the individual, the label is a random and meaningless affliction upon the man; the label is most likely to provoke totally irrational and erroneous assumptions which are themselves enough to inflame fallen man to actions and reactions which they condemn in those who are doing exactly the same thing.

This leads to the issue of hypocrisy, not only with regard to those who judge themselves differently to the manner in which they judge others, but with regard to the behaviour of those who profess Christ to be Lord and saviour. There are those reactions to events display a lack of insight into the nature and expectations of our God which will be a discussed closer to the summit of the mountain. We are confronted, every day, by, or with, tragedy. We feel grief for those who are bereaved and those who are fighting for their lives and their families. We experience despair when confronted by the demand to make difficult and sometimes life-changing choices. The greater tragedy is that tragedies on this scale are occurring on a daily basis globally and are largely ignored. Every day thousands of children die needlessly from starvation, dirty water, and lack of medical treatment; every day Christians and Jews are martyred because of their faith. Every day people in 'civilised' countries are murdered randomly; every day children and women are bought and sold; every day thousands take their own lives because they have lost hope and have no-one to stand with them. Every day children are being seduced into drug habits even 'legally' by big business tobacco companies; every day women are raped in their thousands, in some countries 'legally'

I quote Jeshua again: - "But unless you repent, you too will all perish. Or those eighteen who died when the tower in Siloam fell on them, do you think they were more guilty than all the others living in Jerusalem?"[14] Come on Christians, I use the capital 'C' here to define those who have accepted the conditions of discipleship and are fruit-bearers, we have to see with the mind of Christ, to see from Father's perspective. Jeshua is saying 'Look, stuff happens! Let us get on with it! Has your dad died? Leave the dead to bury the dead!' From Father's perspective all this outpouring of emotion and statements of support and condolence are hypocrisy! His judgement is upon the nations as He has made clear time and time again through the scriptures; 'stuff' will still be happening on a global scale and will be getting worse. We are called to be separate, to be the salt of the earth, to be lights shining in the darkness, to have the mind of Christ, but if we are swayed and influenced to behave in the same manner as the world, we will not be seen for who we are. We do not need to be seen to behave with compassion and love when the world appears to do so, we need to be seen to behave this way consistently otherwise we are just another bunch of hypocrites!

CHAPTER 11

MORE ABOUT ABRAHAM, ISAAC, AND JACOB - AND SEPARATION

It is very tempting to stay in the company of Abraham; his story is full of riches, and we have hardly scratched the surface with regard to what we could glean from this man's testimony, but we have our own path to follow and Father decrees which way we should go and right now we have to resume the upward path.

Our God is known as 'the God of Abraham, Isaac and Jacob'; this declaration was established by God Himself, "Say to the Israelites, 'The Lord, the God of your fathers, the God of Abraham, the God of Isaac and the God of Jacob has sent me to you.' "This is my name forever, the name you shall call me from generation to generation. "Go, assemble the elders of Israel, and say to them, 'The Lord, the God of your fathers, the God of Abraham, Isaac and Jacob appeared to me and said: I have watched over you and have seen what has been done to you in Egypt."[1] This proclamation was repeated to Moses later during his discourse with God: "This," said the Lord, "is so that they may believe that the Lord, the God of their fathers, the God of Abraham, the God of Isaac and the God of Jacob has appeared to you."[2] Jeshua endorsed this eternal truth in Matthew's gospel: "I am the God of Abraham, the God of Isaac, and the God of Jacob, He is not the God of the dead but of the living."[3] By His own testimony He was quoting from scripture as can be ascertained from Matthew: 22:31/32. Peter made the same statement in Acts 3:13. This is a vital revelation for those who erroneously think that Muslims, in particular, worship the same God as us, that is not the case! They, traditionally, are descendants of Ishmael. Ishmael was the son of the bond-servant Hagar, he was born into, and his descendants remain, in bondage; only the descendants of Jacob (Israel) are born with the potential to find freedom whether it is by birth or adoption. The lineage: Abraham, Isaac, Jacob (Israel) is fundamental to God's plan, and it is vital that those who seek the calling of discipleship acknowledge this fact. It is clearly important that we are aware of the lineage through which the chosen nation of Israel was to be established, note that He had said:- "This is my name forever, the name you shall call me from generation to generation." Isaac was the son miraculously conceived by Sarai, the son whom God had promised to Abraham and who was only realised when Abraham came to the end of his own resources. An interesting and significant aside is that one of Abraham's last wishes was that Isaac should not be allowed to return to Ur, the nation of the flesh, out of which Abram had been called so long before.

You can read this in Genesis 24; I am just encouraging a bit of independent study of the scriptures. As for me, I get easily side-tracked, there is so much to feed on in these stories, but I must get back to the study in hand! From Father's perspective this indicates His desire that Abraham's line should remain elect and separate from the nations. Anyway Isaac, as they say, begat Jacob. A fair chunk of Genesis revolves around Jacob, but we shall move straight to chapter 32 which relates that part of his story which is of particular significance in this case. One needs to know that Esau was Jacob's older brother; there had been animosity between them even while they were still in Rebekah's' womb; subsequently Esau had sold his birthright to Jacob for some stew and Jacob had conned Esau out of their father's (Isaac's) blessing. They were not BFF's! Jacob, having been sorely exploited by his Father-in-law Laban and discharged his responsibilities to him, was told by God to return to his homeland.[4] Later Jacob, fearful of Esau and hoping for reconciliation sent messengers.[5] When the messengers returned they did not appear to have good news.[6] Jacob panicked, "In great fear and distress Jacob divided the people who were with him into two groups, and the flocks and herds and camels as well[7] "O God of my father Abraham, God of my father Isaac, Lord, you who said to me, 'Go back to your country and your relatives, and I will make you prosper,"[8] Followed by:- "Save me, I pray, from the hand of my brother Esau, for I am afraid he will come and attack me, and also the mothers with their children."[9] He was obviously not enjoying the prospect of the reunion!

He reacted in the flesh, then he prayed the prayer already quoted, it appears that his faith could not overcome his fear. "That night Jacob got up and took his two wives, his two female servants and his eleven sons and crossed the ford of the Jabbok. After he had sent them across the stream, he sent over all his possessions."[10] This man had sacrificed everything, even, in the end, his wives and children. He had absolutely nothing left, they were all at the mercy of whomsoever came across them. Isolated and vulnerable, it appears that he just sat and waited, no mention of his crying out to the God of Abraham and Isaac, no pleas, only his earlier prayer of thanksgiving and acknowledgement:- "I am unworthy of all the kindness and faithfulness you have shown your servant. I had only my staff when I crossed this Jordan, but now I have become two camps."[11]

"So, Jacob was left alone, and a man wrestled with him till daybreak."[12] Does this not provoke a lot of questioning? Why did God not come to him with solace and comfort? Why not promises of all being well, of safety and restoration? Why not reiterate the promises of prosperity, multitudes of descendants and fatherhood of nations? He, like his granddad before him had lapsed in his faithfulness and tried to do things his own way, motivated by the flesh not the Holy Spirit. Here we see the salient point in this chapter, the awful, magnificent, wrathful, vengeful, self-centred God in pursuit of His own ends wrestles with the man. Of course, God could have totally overwhelmed Jacob in a fraction of a nanosecond, He could have annulled Jacob's privilege of being able to exercise his free-will and forced him into a state of compliance and submission. But He did not! He had plans and they would not be thwarted by the failings of one individual! What was this all about then? Submission! Jacob had, to all intents and purposes, abandoned everything and everyone but had not arrived at the point of submission; he had not, as one of his descendants, King David, had been able to say years later:- "My sacrifice, O God, is a broken spirit; a broken and contrite heart you, God, will not despise."[13] Father is in the business of breaking hearts. This will not appeal to 'pavlova' Christians, but it is true; it is true! If you cannot stand before your God and with a clear conscience and make that statement of truth on your own behalf as Paul did, then you are in trouble "My conscience is clear, but that does not make me innocent. It is the Lord who judges me."[14] I quote Jeshua yet again:- "Not everyone who says to me, 'Lord, Lord,' will enter the kingdom of heaven, but only the one who does the will of my Father who is in heaven."[15] Jacob wrestled all night and suffered a symbol of his brokenness for the rest of his life:- "When the man saw that he could not overpower him, he touched the socket of Jacob's hip so that his hip was wrenched as he wrestled with the man."[16]

This is all so beautiful! See and assimilate another aspect of our paradoxical God:- "When the man saw that he could not overpower him (because that is not the way agapé love works) "He touched the socket of Jacob's hip so that his hip was wrenched as he wrestled with the man." God acknowledged that He could not overpower him. This is so difficult to grasp but is vital for those on the path of discipleship; He could have overpowered Jacob by force, but He chose to overpower him with *love*! We have no idea of what actually went on between God and Jacob, but it is clear that, in the end, Jacob was overcome to the point of submission. "Then the man said, "Let me go, for it is daybreak." But Jacob replied, "I will not let you go unless you bless me."[17] This is the whole point of this particular Word of God: I will wrestle with you and try to overcome you with my love but if you persist in your resistance, I will leave you to suffer the consequences, and there will be no blessing for you! God's response was:- "What is your name?" "Jacob," he answered. Then the man said, "Your name will no longer be Jacob, but Israel, because you have struggled with God and with humans and have overcome." Jacob said, "Please tell me your name." But he replied, "Why do you ask my name?" Then he blessed him there. So, Jacob called the place Peniel, saying, "It is because I saw God face to face, and yet my life was spared."[18]

As I have already confessed, I am easily distracted; I know that the way is upward and, I suppose, we are still going up. But I have to make another, what appears to me, to be a bit of a diversion. I no longer try to figure out what God is up to; I cannot understand His ways and I accept that. I try to practice what I preach, in particular the importance of *only doing what we see the Father doing*, of being totally and only led by the Holy Spirit:- "Jesus gave this answer to the Jews who were harassing Him: "Very truly I tell you, the Son can do nothing by himself; he can do only what he sees his Father doing, because whatever the Father does the Son also does."[19] We are all being conformed to the image of His Son "For those God foreknew he also predestined to be conformed to the image of his Son, that he might be the firstborn among many brothers and sisters."[19] And we are being given the mind of Christ "Who has known the mind of the Lord so as to instruct him?" But we have the mind of Christ."[20] This only applies to disciples! "Why do you call me, 'Lord, Lord,' and do not do what I say? As for everyone who comes to me and hears my words and puts them into practice, I will show you what they are like. They are like a man building a house, who dug down deep and laid the foundation on rock. When a flood came, the torrent struck that house but could not shake it, because it was well built. But the one who hears my words and does not put them into practice is like a man who built a house on the ground without a foundation. The moment the torrent struck that house, it collapsed, and its destruction was complete."[21]

What I am being led by the Spirit to discuss now is the consequences of Jacob's attempts to bring about God's promises through his own fleshy indulgences! I quote again (you can never have too much scripture) "Save me, I pray, from the hand of my brother Esau, for I am afraid he will come and attack me, and also the mothers with their children." Look at this again! He was afraid of his kin who had been born into bondage and was not of the Godly line ordained by his God to be part of His inheritance and was in fear of Him to the extent that he was prepared to abandon everything, including his whole family, and then take on the challenge (although he did not know it at the time) of having to face his God. What we have to face here is the fact that our God is a *divisive* God. (Wow! I did not realize that we were, in fact, heading straight up!) "Do not suppose that I have come to bring peace to the earth. I did not come to bring peace, but a sword. For I have come to turn a man against his father, a daughter against her mother, a daughter-in-law against her mother-in-law."[22] Such an important message that it is repeated in Luke's gospel "Do you think I came to bring peace on earth? No, I tell you, but division."[23]

We indulge, in varying degrees, in the festival known as Christmas. I have to tell you that Christmas is a celebration of a pagan festival and has nothing whatsoever to do with the birth of Christ. It is a celebration of the winter solstice and is celebrated by many pagan religions, it occurs in December and celebrates the shortest day and longest night of the year dependent upon which part of the globe you inhabit. Yeshua would not have been born in December as is verified by much historical and astronomical evidence. It was incorporated into the church of Rome as a celebration as something 'Christian' because it made it more palatable to the multitude of pagans whom Rome was trying to control through religion because they were losing the ability to control by military might. Is this not reminiscent of God's dealings with Jacob? How many are going through the trial of wrestling with God; how many are saying "I have given up everything" Yet Father says "yes but you have not submitted to me, you have not acquiesced to my will. You have not clung on to me until I blessed you, so are you going to revert to the ways of your grandfather and try to do 'stuff' in my name to try and make me more acceptable to the nations? I told Abraham to occupy the 'promised land' but he kept wandering off into Egypt and leaving his inheritance unoccupied! Jacob allowed his fear to bring division, all that he had was split into two camps; there was division in the camp and, in the end, Jacob himself was divided from all his possessions and his stubborn self! This is the way Father works, He selects weak, vulnerable, self-centred, and stubborn individuals, He divides them from everything outside the purposes of His will, effectively discards them, and transforms by overpowering with agapé, they are chosen ones. Ishmael and Esau were both discarded by God, they lapse into relative obscurity whilst God focuses on His purposes; to see the 'God of Abraham, Isaac and Jacob' acknowledged as the one and only true God! He did not rely on the humans, He relied only on His agapé love! This is the character of our Father.

A word to some who are going to fall into the temptation of (mis)quoting some scripture because they do not want to accept truth, as Paul wrote to Timothy "For the time will come when people will not put up with sound doctrine. Instead, to suit their own desires, they will gather around them a great number of teachers to say what their itching ears want to hear."[24] Jesus did not come to bring peace and goodwill to all men! What the heavenly host sang, according to Luke was "Glory to God in the highest heaven, and on earth peace to those on whom his favour rests."[25] Read any good, up-to-date translation, they all say the same, the peace and goodwill to *all* men stuff is rubbish, bordering on blasphemy, distorting the Word of God. If that were the case, where is it? Does scripture lie? Was it for another time? If so, why proclaim it at the birth of the Messiah through the angelic hosts rather than through the words of another prophet? Because the birth was the fulfilment of so many prophesies including those about peace and goodwill. The truth is that the prophesies were not for 'all men' but for God's chosen people. That is why the proclamation was for those on whom His favour rests, or in other translations 'with whom He is pleased'. Jeshua did come to earth as a baby to bring 'goodwill', that is agapé love; He did come to bring 'peace', that is shalom. These are unique words because they can only be experienced by the grace of God, they are beyond the realms of our natural sensibilities and emotions. But they were not to be appropriated at the whim of any man or woman, they can only be experienced through Christ; before Jeshua walked and talked on this earth 'agapé' and 'shalom' were foreign concepts to all but a few, but now they are available to everyone. In this sense they were not 'brought to all men' only made available to them–a different thing entirely!

During the time that Paul and Silas were in a stinking Roman jail a miracle occurred which terrified the jailer. Note that they were all in the jail, jailed or jailer, they were all in the same boat (well, the same jail actually) Paul and Silas knew all about agapé and shalom but the jailer did not! Like Jacob he was a slave to his own fear. "He then brought them out and asked, "Sirs, what must I do to be saved?" They replied, "Believe in the Lord Jesus, and you will be saved, you and your household."[26] But this is only the start, we are required not only to accept Jesus as our Saviour but to install Him in our lives as Lord! Jeshua said: - "Not everyone who says to me, 'Lord, Lord,' will enter the kingdom of heaven, but only the one who does the will of my Father who is in heaven."[27] We cannot put Christ back into Christmas as proposed by some well-intentioned but misguided individuals because He was never in it! He is the same yesterday today and forever[28] He is never 'in' or 'out' of any particular day or celebration; if we are a disciple, He lives in us every day, He does not change. We cannot celebrate Him any differently on any particular day or even on the basis of an emotional whim. If this is not the case then something is wrong, that is why Paul rebuked the Galatians: "But now that you know God, or rather are known by God, how is it that you are turning back to those weak and miserable forces? Do you wish to be enslaved by them all over again? You are observing special days and months and seasons and years! I fear for you, that somehow, I have wasted my efforts on you."[29]

Is Father wasting His efforts on you?

CHAPTER 12

WAITING FOR THE GUIDE

I am not inclined to indulge in a 'Christmas dinner'; I used to; it is only recently that Father has dealt with my propensity for indulgence in food. As I start to write this the Holy Spirit is starting to lead me onto the subject of self-indulgence and self-discipline. When He (the Holy Spirit) gave me the subtitle for this chapter I had no idea that we were going in this direction. I think the guide has arrived! Being a bit of a non-conformist, I am inclined to be a bit cheeky sometimes and call upon our wonderful Father to let me in on some of His secrets; we were just seeing You wrestle with Jacob and change his name to Israel, now You are leading us off somewhere which is, apparently, unrelated, at least in the direct sense! However, Thy will be done! I suppose as we head higher up the mountain it becomes more and more necessary to shed unnecessary baggage and lighten one's load; in fact, it is essential! We, if you are still with me, are on the path of discipleship, a bit like 'Pilgrims Progress' but more demanding. This is not presumption on my part, I believe in the essential and adequate function of all ministries, but discipleship is not specified, although inferred, in Bunyan's tale. My function is to stress not the difficulties of the way, but the purpose of it! "In the same way, those of you who do not give up everything you have cannot be my disciples."[1] And whoever does not carry their cross and follow me cannot be my disciple."[2]

This is why the subject of discipline arises, self-discipline and self-control. For my own part I was brought to the place of salvation, the foot of the cross, having been thoroughly convicted of my sin; I was not a drug addict, an alcoholic, a wife or child-beater, a thief, or a murderer who had had good reason to seek redemption, just a regular guy, or so I thought! I led a sheltered life, good education, gainfully employed, delightfully married and generally an altogether pretty decent bloke! How was it that I was under such awful conviction that, in God's eyes, I was not one jot different from proper sinners, the likes of Pharaoh, Nebuchadnezzar, Caligula, Attila the Hun, Hitler or Pol Pot? I had not behaved in any wise like any of these; nor, in my opinion, qualified as any of the aforementioned 'proper sinners.'

Let us go back a little way and consider Father's dealings with Abraham and Isaac again. He just chose us, that is all, we cannot figure it out; He just chose us, all of us, that is all! There is absolutely no point in trying to figure out why; the reason is that He is going to have His own way, provide a bride for His Son, and no-one is going to thwart His perfect plan. Somehow, He is going to make His own selection based solely on His grace and He will work to make, if He deems it prudent to do so, even the most unsavoury and unsalvable people individuals to befit the bride of Christ! If He chooses to include me in His scheme, then Hallelujah! Just another sinner, convicted of sin and saved by grace. I have often compared my testimony with those of ex-addicts, reformed criminals, and satan-worshippers; people who can testify to a drastic change in their behaviour but always considered my own experience pretty unspectacular and not really worth mentioning, but now I realise that my testimony rests solely on my conviction of sin. If you have been doing the sort of stuff mentioned you must be pretty aware that you fall well into the category of 'sinner', for my part I never considered myself one! As we are heading upwards, we need to pay attention to that facet of God's character which states that He does not care who we are or have been, His only interest is in the fact that His will is being done, as is prayed by millions every day, and His Church is being assembled strictly according to His design.

To be called is one thing, to be chosen is another, remember Jeshua said that "many are invited, but few are chosen."[3] The calling is not the be-all and end-all, God's will is that once called we should pursue the path of discipleship "In the same way, those of you who do not give up everything you have cannot be my disciples."[4] "Not everyone who says to me, 'Lord, Lord,' will enter the kingdom of heaven, but only the one who does the will of my Father who is in heaven."[5] There are many deluded and deceived individuals who adopt the doctrine of unlimited grace and continue to behave as abominably as they have always done. They would do well to consider the whole nature of God and seek Him to bring them to the place of repentance! It is apparent that many will be denied the Kingdom in spite of having called Him 'Lord.' There are also those who will only scrape in by the skin of their teeth as testified by Paul: "For no one can lay any foundation other than the one already laid, which is Jesus Christ. If anyone builds on this foundation using gold, silver, costly stones, wood, hay or straw, their work will be shown for what it is, because the Day will bring it to light. It will be revealed with fire, and the fire will test the quality of each person's work. If what has been built survives, the builder will receive a reward."[6] There are many who are convinced that they are 'once and for all saved' but this is clearly not the case, even those who are in a state of salvation but insist on presuming that they can continue to pursue their own fleshy ambitions 'in the name of Christ'. They do not think that they will be accountable on judgement day and have no incentive to earnestly seek the will of the Father to see if there is any need seek spiritual help in the realms of self-discipline and self-control.

At this juncture I have to point out that the previous 1000 or so words have been lying dormant somewhere in the guts of my computer for quite a while. As I have stated before, I endeavour to practice what I preach, I am academic by nature and would not find it too difficult to write an essay based only on scripture but "He has made us competent as ministers of a new covenant, not of the letter but of the Spirit; for the letter kills, but the Spirit gives life."[7] I do not presume that what 'comes off the nib of my pen' has the anointing of the Holy Spirit; only after an appropriate time of 'being still and knowing that He is God' do I deign to put pen to paper (actually- finger tips to keyboard). Having been waiting for so long and actually forgotten that this part is subtitled "Waiting for the Guide", today I had decided that I had started to move up the mountain having taken the wrong trail. I fired up the ol' laptop with the intent of deleting all that had been written and waiting on the Spirit to inspire new thoughts. Just before I did so I was given another subtitle; "Is There a Better Way?". As I re-read the first few paragraphs, I realized that this might be a rhetorical question. Yes! There is a better way! That way is to be led entirely by the Holy Spirit so that He can make us more like Christ. This is not an option! "For those God foreknew he also predestined to be *conformed to the image of his Son*, that he might be the firstborn among many brothers and sisters."[8] Whoever claims to live in him must live as Jesus did."[9] The word translated 'must' in this version is also translated 'ought' or 'is obligated'. There is no doubt that 'the better way' is Christlikeness and is obligatory!

Earlier in the chapter I stressed the necessity of shedding baggage, I also have a passion for those who call Jeshua 'Lord' but will not enter the Kingdom because they do not do the will of the Father[10] We are all called to make disciples, *not* 'followers' and we are encouraged in this ministry by James: "My brothers and sisters, if one of you should wander from the truth and someone should bring that person back, remember this: Whoever turns a sinner from the error of their way will save them from death and cover over a multitude of sins."[11] If we are to continue up the mountain and decide to shed the baggage of sin on the way up we need to know exactly what sin is. Sin, according to the scriptures is 'anything that that does not come from faith', i.e. presumption; "But whoever has doubts is condemned if they eat, because their eating is not from faith; and everything that does not come from faith is sin."[12] Now to him who is able to establish you in accordance with my gospel, the message I proclaim about Jesus Christ, in keeping with the revelation of the mystery hidden for long ages past, but now revealed and made known through the prophetic writings by the command of the eternal God, so that all the Gentiles might come to the obedience that comes from faith to the only wise God be glory forever through Jesus Christ! Amen."[13]

And "Consequently, faith comes from hearing the message, and the message is heard through the word of Christ." (Some translations 'God')[14]

N.B. The 'word' used here is 'rhemata'; this specifically refers to the spoken word, that God-breathed word that comes directly out of the mouth of the Holy Spirit and into the spirit of the individual. This is the word out of which the faith to which Paul was referring is manifest, when the Holy Spirit speaks *and* one listens (that, sadly, is often not the case) one is given knowledge that only comes from personal experience, of having heard God speak on a personal level, it is part of the experience of the listener. Paul uses mainly two words in the original Greek which are both translated 'knowledge' one is 'gnosis' which is best described as 'head-knowledge' such as 2+2=4, Paris is the capital of France or lead is more dense than aluminium. The other is 'epignosis' which is entirely different, this comes from an experiential event, one in which the individual has participated such as giving birth, hitting a thumb with a hammer, going on a holiday or, best of all, being born again! Those who are in danger of either not getting into the Kingdom at all or, at best, having much of their work burnt up in the fire, are well advised to consider whether what they are doing is of faith, whether what they are doing is inspired by epignosis of what the will of the Father is, or whether it is born of the flesh, that is, sin. Faith and presumption are poles apart, whatever is not of faith is presumption, sin, 'good works' are not in themselves of value in God's judgement. "All of us have become like one who is unclean, and all our righteous acts are like filthy rags; we all shrivel up like a leaf, and like the wind our sins sweep us away."[15] It transpires that, even when they were actually trying hard, Israel's efforts were not acceptable to God: "Brothers and sisters, my heart's desire and prayer to God for the Israelites is that they may be saved. For I can testify about them that they are zealous for God, but their zeal is not based on knowledge (epignosis!). Since they did not know the righteousness of God and sought to establish their own, they did not submit to God's righteousness."[16]

Their folly was that they sought to establish their own righteousness! This is not God's way, Jeshua told us to "seek *first* his kingdom and *His* righteousness, and all these things will be given to you as well."[17] That is why we are expected to fulfil the role of disciple and give up everything, being zealous is not good enough. Father does appreciate our good works:- "For we are God's handiwork, created in Christ Jesus to do good works, which God prepared in advance for us to do."[18] "For this reason, since the day we heard about you, we have not stopped praying for you. We continually ask God to fill you with the knowledge of his will through all the wisdom and understanding that the Spirit gives, so that you may live a life worthy of the Lord and please him in every way: bearing fruit in every good work, growing in the knowledge of God."[19] But note that these are not works of self-righteousness, self-justification or self-gratification; they are works wrought out of *His* righteousness; works inspired by the indwelling of the Holy Spirit, they are the fruit of the Spirit! Anything else is 'filthy rags!' Remember God does not *need* us to do anything! We are aware that He is omnipotent and can do whatsoever He likes. He does not need us to *do* anything; then "what is the point?" you may well ask. This is where we take a significant stride further upwards towards the mountain summit. The point is that, in His wisdom, He elects to use us to perform 'good works' on His behalf; we do not 'do' good works or, more precisely, bear spiritual fruit, He does the works through us. He causes us to be fruit-bearers and all for His glory, Jeshua told us "let your light shine before others, that they may see your good deeds and glorify your Father in heaven."[20] and "Live such good lives among the pagans that, though they accuse you of doing wrong, they may see your good deeds and glorify God on the day he visits us."[21]

The Spirit-filled person, the disciple, the truly repentant, dead to the flesh, and truly born-again person has no need to 'do good works', to do stuff for God; he/she *is* a good work, he/she cannot help but bear fruit, there is no effort or striving involved, it all comes (super)naturally! (This is how the believer can experience 'shalom' - exquisite contentment). There have been, and are, a multitude of prophesies regarding the state of the church and Father's attitude towards it. Some time ago I was told that He is sick of a sick church; today the language is harsher, He is dealing with an apostate church. Note well! He is dealing with an apostate church. Vanity and self-righteousness are rife. No denomination or sect is immune; indeed, it is some of those who pride themselves on 'having got it all (or most of it) right who are the worst offenders. Consider those who move in cliques with total disregard for true fellowship, those who manifest the 'holier than thou' spirit of vanity and pride. Those who will execute programs for third-world countries, new buildings, initiate conferences, commission T.V. programs and all sorts of other 'stuff' but have never hugged a smelly alcoholic, an unshaven homeless person, or a distraught teenager; who have never washed another's feet or deemed it not within their 'remit' to clean toilets; it is beneath the dignity of some to even give up a little time to wait on tables. So many of these are contenders for, at best, having most of their 'stuff' burnt up in the fire and only 'narrowly escaping as through the flames'[22].

We are told: - "Whatever you do, work heartily, as for the Lord and not for men."[23] This applies to oneself, self is number one man (or woman), does whatever you are doing make you just 'feel good'? Does it help you feel justified? Do you get even one iota of pride in feeling that you 'did something for God? If it was not done 'whole-heartedly' only for the glory of God, if your 'good work' was not at the behest of the Holy Spirit, if you did not have epignosis that this was His will then it is filthy rags and of no value. All works of the flesh! "So, I say, walk by the Spirit, and you will not gratify the desires of the flesh."[23]

Yes! There is a better way, wait for the guide! Waiting demands abandonment of self-indulgence and application of self-discipline. Jeshua said: - "I am going to send you what my Father has promised; but stay in the city until you have been clothed with power from on high."[25] Being clothed with power from on high is a matter of epignosis. It does not come, necessarily, by the 'laying on of hands' nor by indulgence in any rite, including that of participating in an 'altar-call'. I am going to revise from the book of Acts:- "When the day of Pentecost came, they were all together in one place. Suddenly a sound like the blowing of a violent wind came from heaven and filled the whole house where they were sitting. They saw what seemed to be tongues of fire that separated and came to rest on each of them. All of them were filled with the Holy Spirit and began to speak in other tongues as the Spirit enabled them."[26] The filling of the Holy Spirit is clearly a sovereign act of the Holy Spirit Himself, He does not arrive at the behest of any man. "The wind blows wherever it pleases. You hear its sound, but you cannot tell where it comes from or where it is going. So it is with everyone born of the Spirit."[27] Some observations regarding this phenomenon; First: In Luke 24 Jeshua was addressing disciples (remember the definition), we can infer that they included the Eleven, Mary Magdalene, Joanna, Mary mother of James, Peter, Cleopas, John, James, Andrew, Philip, Thomas, Bartholomew, Matthew, James, son of Alphaeus, Simon and Judas son of James. Only at this juncture, after His resurrection, did He open their minds to understand the Scriptures. "However, as it is written: "What no eye has seen, what no ear has heard, and what no human mind has conceived, the things God has prepared for those who love him these are the things God has revealed to us by his Spirit. The Spirit searches all things, even the deep things of God."[28]

"At that time Jesus said, "I praise you, Father, Lord of heaven and earth, because you have hidden these things from the wise and learned and revealed them to little children."[29] These things are a salutary lesson for some of those described above who profess to be teachers, but have not had their minds opened by the Holy Spirit yet presume to teach out of the flesh. What is taught may appear to be sound doctrine and Scriptural but that which is born of the flesh will all be burned up, if you presume to be a teacher, prophet or aught else without having epignosis of your calling then you are a false minister. Having gnosis, academic knowledge, of scripture falls short of the glory of God and is of no profit to anyone. "But the wisdom that comes from heaven is first of all pure; then peace-loving, considerate, submissive, full of mercy and good fruit, impartial and sincere."[30] Not bombastic, self-aggrandising, presumptuous, pretentious, nor focused on anyone but the Father. They were told to wait in the city, they had only been told to expect the fulfilment of one of God's promises and be blessed, that was it! But they were obedient! They did not emulate our dear father Abraham and try to anticipate God, they only did as they were told like Jeshua in John 5:19, only what He saw the Father doing, no more, no less! They followed good scriptural adage and were still and knew that He was God.[31] Those that wait on the Lord will renew their strength and soar on wings like eagles."[32] Obedience is better than sacrifice.[33] Obedience, being still and renewing are all part of the ever increasingly difficult ascent of the mountain. All involve the annihilation of self-(indulgence) and investiture of self-discipline. Then these were all people 'off the street' something they had in common was that they had become child-like, not insofar as they were naïve and simple, but they had the openness of mind to assimilate spiritual truth without prejudice.

To appreciate the ministry of the Holy Spirit and the epignosis of Him and His power and role in the life of the individual, we need to appraise the condition of those who were so blessed on this pentecostal occasion. We know, apart from the fact that they all qualified as disciples as defined by the Messiah Himself having given up everything to follow Him, that they further commended themselves by their act of obedience and already evidenced the fruit of the Spirit by which they would later become known.[34] It would seem that the Holy Spirit was able to 'fill' them because they had already emptied themselves of 'self'. This would be the only virtue common to all those assembled in the upper room that day. I revealed earlier that I came under an awful conviction of my sin. I was in a room full of people (how I got there is another story) but, so far as I was concerned, I might just as well have been in there on my own with just the preacher, who I had never met before, or since. Every word that came out of his mouth was an indictment of my abhorrent state, nothing about me had any virtue or worth whatsoever; after some time of this excruciation, I was a total wreck. I was sitting right at the back (guess why) and might well have been quivering and shaking with fear, I do not know, it was never commented on; so I guess Father, in His mercy, did save me some embarrassment.

I knew that I just had to get down to the front if I was to be relieved of all this condemnation, I was under such awful conviction that I would have done anything in order to try and get there. I would have assaulted the whole Russian army, (they were the big threat at the time) would have tried to swim the Atlantic, crawled through a pit of venomous snakes, or taken on a whole jungle of ferocious beasts; I would have done *anything*! The point of that this part of my testimony is that I have epignosis of having died! I *died*! At this point my testimony tends to corroborate those who have had literal 'death' experiences, except for the intense white light my story is similar. I have no idea where I was for the next two hours, apparently my body was on the floor, but my spirit was on a grand tour. I have seen the gates of hell, which I would never attempt to describe, and also experienced some of heaven. I would not try to explain that either, except to say that I experienced something which is common to many other testimonies. Somewhere along the way I had this incredible awareness of being baptised, that is, totally immersed and infused by what can only ever be described as warm liquid love; it seems that no-one can come up with a better description, not in English anyway. After years of prayer, being still and knowing that He is God, I have come to the conclusion that the Holy Spirit can, or will, only fill us to the extent that we have died to self. The disciple is one who has died to self; the one who has died to self will bear fruit, this is Father's way and His only way. We are told that we are being made Christ-like and that the only way we will be known with any degree of validity is by the fruit we bear; I wonder if we were to hold a survey of all the members of our so-called churches how many would be publicly recognised as fruit-bearers? I grow weary, this has been a particularly strenuous stretch of the mountain to climb.

One or two closing thoughts:- Focus only on the Lord Jeshua, do not become followers of Paul, Apollos or Cephas.[35]

Focus on a personality is unscriptural, unhealthy and can be positively dangerous. Be a Berean[36] and check out everything with the Scriptures; this is why we need to die to self and make more room for the Holy Spirit. Pray for the gift of discernment, same argument, your gift of discernment is only as reliable as the reality of your death. You are probably embroiled in an apostate church and God's judgement is going to be soon manifest upon it. Your gift of discernment is critical if you desire to know father's will, if you cannot tell His voice from your own, or some vain and presumptuous human, or that of the enemy, you are in trouble, aren't you?

Do not be followers of the spectacular. Even some of those who have performed wonders in His name will be told:- "Many will say to me on that day, 'Lord, Lord, did we not prophesy in your name and in your name drive out demons and, in your name, perform many miracles?' Then I will tell them plainly, 'I never knew you. Away from me, you evildoers!'"[37] Jeshua never denied that they had done these things in His name, but they clearly did not fulfil all the conditions, God will use anyone or anything for His glory, He does not care! Having a spectacular 'ministry' does not reflect any virtue on the part of the minister if he/she is not a fruit bearer. This will come as nasty shock to many, read the small print! *All* Scripture is still wholly relevant, but it requires an opening of mind on the part of the Holy Spirit to reveal it.

Remember the whole substance of this part of the message:- *WAIT FOR THE GUIDE- HE WILL SHOW YOU A BETTER WAY!*

CHAPTER 13

A Little Embellishment - About Love and Judgement

On having retraced the steps taken in chapter 12 a few times (as is my wont) I am inclined to embellish a little before heading directly upwards again. Having got this far up and embraced the company of the guide, what we now know is that we must be seeking a better way, or as is otherwise translated, 'most excellent way', 'a way of life that is best of all', 'a more excellent way', 'a way that is beyond comparison', or 'a more surpassing way'.[1] What we are seeking on this venture is a deeper understanding of our Heavenly Father and, hopefully, our relationship with him. This 'way', which qualifies for every superlative there is, is Jeshua, the Christ; He *is* the way!

He said:- "I am the way and the truth and the life. No one comes to the Father except through me."[2] One of the things I emphasised in chapter 12 was the fact that God does not rely on any of our supposed virtues to qualify us to be used by Him for His purposes. Abraham, Jacob, and myself are testimony to the way that God will, apparently, randomly select individuals of no virtue and work with them to bring them to the place where, purely and only motivated by agapé love and the desire to be obedient and glorify Him, they will be used by Him for His purposes. "In him we were also chosen, having been predestined according to the plan of him who works out everything in conformity with the purpose of his will."[3] Therefore we can have no pride in how we are used or what we are used for. "But will confine our boasting to the sphere of service God himself has assigned to us, a sphere that also includes you."[4] "Do not think of yourself more highly than you ought, but rather think of yourself with sober judgement, in accordance with the faith God has distributed to each of you."[5] One aspect of the fruit of the Holy Spirit is humbleness. Please do not resort to Galatians 5:22 and conclude that humbleness is not included. The first in the list of evidence of Holy Spirit fruit-bearing is love (agapé) This is singular! *One* fruit! Agape is synonymous with Christlikeness! Jeshua is God and God is agape.[6] Joy, peace etcetera are all aspects of the one fruit. To explain this, consider an apple; I say, "here is an apple:- stem, peel, flesh, juice, pips, core, sugar, proteins, enzymes." I could go on and on in greater and greater detail describing the whole apple. But it is only one apple, there is only one fruit! One of the attributes to be included is humbleness. Humbleness is referred to many, many times in Scripture; here are a couple of quotes to enforce the need to recognise humbleness as part of the fruit. "For the Lord takes delight in his people; he crowns the humble with victory"[7] "Be completely humble and gentle; be patient, bearing with one another in love."[8] "Humble yourselves before the Lord, and he will lift you up."[9] Vanity and arrogance are rife among the congregations and are abhorrent to the Father, the consequence of indulgence in these vices is a judgemental spirit, this results in disunity and intolerance, they are all fodder for the ego and the enemy! "Do not judge, or you too will be judged. For in the same way you judge others, you will be judged, and with the measure you use, it will be measured to you. "Why do you look at the speck of sawdust in your brother's eye and pay no attention to the plank in your own eye?"[10] This is patently clear and not open to discussion, the Words of Christ are explicit! This is not the same as what Paul is saying to the Corinthians: "The person with the Spirit makes judgements about all things, but such a person is not subject to merely human judgements,".[11] What is being stated here regards *the person with the Spirit*! Such a person would be employing the gifts of discernment, wisdom, revelation, and discrimination as deemed appropriate by the Holy Spirit; he would only be judging in the sense of evaluating and assessing the circumstances and the behaviour of those with whom he is involved, he is not passing judgement on any person!

P.S. This P.S. is written over a year after the rest of this chapter. I guess I must have been waiting and listening for guidance on how I was to proceed with the word; but, it seems, nothing was forthcoming and eventually I must have concluded that we had all got as far as we could go in company, and that Father's will was that we should either rest where we were or continue to seek a path to greater heights, but only in the company of our personal guide. And so, chapter 13 has been nestling among some boulders in a high, rocky place unread, but there to be dusted off and, if need be, elaborated upon when God deemed it the right time to do so. This is the day that the Lord has made, let us rejoice and be glad in it! It appears that the time has come to take up keyboard and paper and share some more of what Father has been saying to me.

CHAPTER 14

SOME MUSINGS FROM HIGH PLACES - CONSIDERING FAIRNESS AND JUSTICE

I had been quite ill for some weeks, totally incapacitated, no desire or initiative to even get out of bed for the most part; a most debilitating and energy-sapping affliction. It has been fairly widespread and will be very familiar, certainly to those who gave experienced it and also to those who are close to someone who has. I have been literally weeks on antibiotics and steroids, some of the side-effects of which are not a lot less unpleasant than the affliction itself. I only share this because it is so relevant to the context of this chapter as is the book of Habakkuk, "The Sovereign Lord is my strength; he makes my feet like hinds' feet on high places."

Few things excite me as much as sitting down at the keyboard or being aware that I am being called to testify orally and to just wait on the Holy Spirit for His guidance. When God is feasting you with revelation it is too easy to allow the flesh to quench the Spirit and for *you* to take over and start to say the things that *you* want to say, be they of sound doctrine or not! This is a case, frequently witnessed, of our filthy rags being waved about in the breeze under the illusion that they are banners for Christ. Sometimes it will take me days to write just a few sentences, sometimes I will write pages at a sitting but only at His behest will I commit to any statement. This is part of my policy of staying in Gods' shalom and maintaining, like Paul, a clear conscience before God. There is nothing 'super-spiritual' about this; this is the normal Christian life, study the scriptures with diligence! It is important that chronology and coherence are maintained in the interests of the integrity of the Word, so this post, I think, will be bit like Habakkuk's, a sequential narrative. So, to start at the beginning, I refer to my rather abrupt (overnight) exodus from my various activities and commitments as my being 'withdrawn from active service'. This is not the first time I have been withdrawn from active service; taken from the hurley-burley of daily 'normal' life and closeted practically alone, in a quiet and still place, sometimes for weeks at a time (40 days and 40 nights come to mind but I am not counting, and there are no indicators on my calendar). Every single activity in which I was involved was excluded, it was not really that much of a surprise as I had seen God start to curtail my involvement with some of the activities in which I was participant. Anyway, at this point I must restate some vital and eternal truths: -Romans 8:28 "And we know that *in all things* God works for the good of those who love him, who have been called according to *his* purpose.

Ephesians 1:11 "In him we were also chosen, having been predestined according to the plan of him who works out *everything* in conformity with the purpose of his will."

Malachi 3:6 "I the *Lord do not change*. So you, the descendants of Jacob, are not destroyed."

Deuteronomy 4:2 "Do not add to what I command you and do not subtract from it but keep the commands of the Lord your God that I give you."

James 1:17 "Every good and perfect gift is from above, coming down from the Father of the heavenly lights, *who does not change like shifting shadows.*

I emphasise:- He works out everything in conformity with the of His will, He does not change, and all of His word is always relevant! No part of His Word moves in or out of relevance according to the time of day or anything else! This is because part of my testimony is that God put me flat on my back and I am fed up with 'pavlova' Christians telling me that God doesn't do that anymore! "As he went along, he saw a man blind from birth. His disciples asked him, "Rabbi, who sinned, this man or his parents, that he was born blind?" "Neither this man nor his parents sinned," said Jesus, "but this happened so that the works of God might be displayed in him."[2] Read the scriptures with diligence! I shall be relying on my dear brother Habakkuk quite a bit, so I shall quote him here:- "His splendour was like the sunrise; rays flashed from his hand, where his power was hidden. Plague went before him; pestilence followed his steps. He stood, and shook the earth; he looked, and made the nations tremble. The ancient mountains crumbled, and the age-old hills collapsed, but he marches on forever. I saw the tents of Cushan in distress, the dwellings of Midian in anguish."[3] This same sentiment is expressed over and over again in scripture, God will do whatsoever He pleases and is absolutely justified in doing so! We have established this for a fact a long way down, on the lower slopes!

Having been rendered, to all intents and purposes, physically inert, it did not affect my spiritual state; God had put me flat on my back because he wanted to have some private time away from all distractions. This is the purpose of being taken into the wilderness! My role as intercessor was accentuated, much time was spent just praying in the Spirit[4,5] I am led to appeal to my brothers and sisters to consider 'volunteering' as intercessors. It is lonely, painful, sometimes exhausting and leaves no space for self-indulgence or self-aggrandising; there is none of the glamour or assent which goes with 'down the front' ministries yet it is the most crucial and anointed of all the functions incorporated in the Body of Christ. "Rejoice always, pray continually, give thanks in all circumstances; for this is God's will for you in Christ Jesus."[6] So many of the saints will testify that prayer is the foundation upon which the Church flourishes, without prayer there will be nothing of value. Sometimes, during the first couple of weeks I would violate my own credo and enquire of the Father "at my age and with this type of infection has my time come?" He works with me on a 'need to know' basis, why was I not surprised when I did not get an answer? Eventually it dawned on me that it was probably not, in fact, 'my time' yet. Later, during the course of my sojourn, Father began to give me a word; "I give you feet as hinds' feet on high places." This exact phrase was given several times over a number of days. Eventually, during one of my more 'with it' moments I got up and looked up the scripture. It is used twice by King David, as part of his song of praise recorded in 2 Samuel 22:33 and again in Psalm 18:33. However my attention was focused on Habakkuk who, a few hundred years later, employed the same phrase at the end of his prayer, the conclusion of his writings. I think it was at this stage that I began to feel quite excited and became aware of the anointing, and that this was of some significance although there was no indication of its relevance to, what has turned out to be this book, at the time.

Please stroll with me through the writings of Habakkuk and reflect on the relevance of his prophetic word for our day. I have, during the time of sojourn, been taken through the whole gamut of Habakkuk's revelations and had them made clear and relevant on a personal level. Of necessity I quote significant portions of Habakkuk in order that my words should be fully qualified by his witness. "How long, Lord, must I call for help, but you do not listen? Or cry out to you, "Violence!" but you do not save? Why do you make me look at injustice? Why do you tolerate wrongdoing? Destruction and violence are before me; there is strife, and conflict abounds. Therefore, the law is paralysed, and justice never prevails. The wicked hem in the righteous, so that justice is perverted."[7] Do you look around and gasp at the news? Do you gaze in amazement at the condition of the world? Do you despair at the corruption, injustices, sedition, and diabolical indulgences that permeate every one of the various societies in which we live? If you are already an intercessor, do you cry out to our God for days and nights at a time on behalf of the state of this world? Do you lift your head, look around, observe the same degeneration, increase in decadence, the inflation of degeneracy and the flourishing of all things foul and evil? Read verse 2 again. Do you scratch about and search in vain for what you hope will be God's answer or do you instead see things falling further apart all around you, especially at a personal level?

Do you, as did I, ask the same question as Habakkuk? On the 'need to know' basis Father has blessed? me with some revelations endorsed by and witnessed by Habakkuk. All this, of course, is prophetic; the role of prophet is not to be coveted, it is a burden which cannot be shouldered with a careless spirit nor is it an appointment to be cast upon the frivolous or irresponsible. "The one who prophesies speaks to people for their strengthening, encouraging and comfort."[8] Sadly this is so often taken in isolation as no scripture should be, and is taught in isolation by false teachers. This is only a small part of the role of the prophet and the function of prophesy. The role of the prophet is far more often to teach, rebuke, correct and train in righteousness and he, or she, frequently suffers dreadfully, even unto death at the hands of those who aught have been strengthened, encouraged, and comforted, according to Fathers' approbative will, by the Word.

Take note, belovéd, "Look at the nations and watch and be utterly amazed. For I am going to do something in your days that you would not believe, even if you were told."[9] I have been sharing this for some time; we are in the throes of a big shake-up, God is dealing with an apostate church, we are experiencing the consequences of our Babylonian lifestyle. As many others, globally, have prophesied- we are again living in Babylon! I say, "Keep the oil levels on 'full', keep the wicks of the lamps immaculately trimmed, take a deep breath, and keep your head down- you aint seen nothin' yet!" "If anyone has ears to hear, let them hear."[10] "I am raising up the Babylonians, that ruthless and impetuous people, who sweep across the whole earth to seize dwellings not their own."[11] Remember that Nebuchadnezzar was appointed by God. "Now I will give all your countries into the hands of my servant Nebuchadnezzar king of Babylon; I will make even the wild animals subject to him."[12] Albeit that Nebuchadnezzar, after his having exercised God's judgement on the Southern Kingdom, he, himself, suffered God's judgement! So it is with the case of God's judgement being brought to bear upon the nations. The nations will exercise God's judgement upon his whole creation, including the apostate church then the nations will be subject to His judgement themselves.

Do not be surprised at this teaching; the pattern is already well established; it is endorsed in prophesy and manifest explicitly in His dealings with Judah in exile. The apostate Judeans were carted off into Babylon where they rapidly assimilated themselves into the pagan society. They maintained their theocratic identity but soon compromised their integrity by adopting the Babylonian lifestyle, in many cases thriving in it. That is why only a remnant were led back to restore the temple, the majority of the Judeans stayed behind to indulge in their tastes for things Babylonian. This is particularly relevant: the whole of Judah was taken into exile, there were no exceptions as in the case of Noah or Abram, made on the grounds of obedience being considered as righteousness. Even those who were to emerge as the remnant with their faith(fulness) more or less intact were subject to the horrors of Babylon, they were not exempt! Remember God uses trial and tribulation to refine and perfect! Do these words make you uncomfortable? If they do, recall the words of James:- "Consider it pure joy, my brothers and sisters, whenever you face trials of many kinds, because you know that the testing of your faith produces perseverance. Let perseverance finish its work so that you may be mature and complete, not lacking anything."[13]

Habakkuk, having had his first complaint addressed by Father, revealing that He was going to use the Babylonians, and the fact that ' I am was going to do something in your days that you would not believe, even if you were told,' again seeks the Word of the Lord. I believe Habakkuk to have been motivated only, as am I, by a desire for a greater understanding of his God and a deepening of his relationship with Him. I do not discern any challenge, any questioning, or any lack of acceptance of God's will in the content of his discourse. This passage is headed 'Habakkuk's 'Second Complaint' in my Bible, I feel that the man is being somewhat slighted by this. I shall now quote:- "Lord, are you not from everlasting? My God, my Holy One, you will never die. You, Lord, have appointed them to execute judgement; you, my Rock, have ordained them to punish. Your eyes are too pure to look on evil; you cannot tolerate wrongdoing. Why then do you tolerate the treacherous? Why are you silent while the wicked swallow up those more righteous than themselves? You have made people like the fish in the sea, like the sea creatures that have no ruler. The wicked foe pulls all of them up with hooks, he catches them in his net, he gathers them up in his dragnet; and so, he rejoices and is glad. Therefore, he sacrifices to his net and burns incense to his dragnet, for by his net he lives in luxury and enjoys the choicest food. Is he to keep on emptying his net, destroying nations without mercy?"[14] Sorry but I did warn you! ☺

My transliteration:- "Father God are you not the most amazing, immaculate, infallible, and perfect being? you are eternal, and you created us in your likeness therefore you will not let us who are the children of Abraham, perish. You are the author and creator of everything, you codified the whole law, including the Torah, which governs every facet of your creation. The law is yours and you will judge by it, which is your divine prerogative, this is the definition of justice. What is perceived as 'fair' or otherwise is inconsequential, *justice is justice!* You have raised up nations and individuals to dispense your justice. O rock, you who are utterly stable, consistent, unchanging, and utterly reliable, and you choose to dispense your justice in this manner. Your plan is perfect, and you are infallible. You made me to look upon these things but how can you, in your purity, look upon these things? You have allowed mankind to be swept about this way like fish floundering in the sea with no direction. Are you going to allow these things to continue? The evil one praises and worships himself with indulgence in the affluence and wealth which does not rightly belong to him, are you really going to continue to allow him to do so? You are perfect, pure, holy, unimpeachable, and immaculate; it is O.K. for the likes of me to look upon these things but how can you bear it? This is part of the paradoxical nature of our God which was discussed on the lower slopes, it is a fact that our Holiest of Holy gods will raise up Pharaohs and Nebuchadnezzars, He will send famine, plague, and pestilence, He will strike down armies in their thousands, innocents will have to suffer, and the wicked will flourish. We just have to deal with it! As Habakkuk will reveal shortly; "I will stand at my watch and station myself on the ramparts; I will look to see what he will say to me, and what answer I am to give to this complaint."[15] As will I.

"Then the Lord replied: "Write down the revelation and make it plain on tablets so that a herald may run with it. For the revelation awaits an appointed time; it speaks of the end and will not prove false. Though it linger, wait for it; it will certainly come and will not delay."[16] Let us consider the role of prophet and prophesy a little further before moving on. "He has made us competent as ministers of a new covenant, not of the letter but of the Spirit; for the letter kills, but the Spirit gives life."[17] *The letter kills!* So much confusion is generated, so much false teaching propagated and so much power conceded to the enemy because the letter is employed in favour of the Spirit. Translations, interpretations and exegeses and transliterations are proliferated but scripture tells us that we should be listening and reading only in the Spirit and even then, we must be wary. A good place to start is with the fact that, in spite of all the scriptures identifying Jeshua as the Messiah, the fact remained unacknowledged until the Holy Spirit revealed the truth to Peter[18] Only just before the ascension did He open their minds to understand the scriptures.[19] "This is what we speak, not in words taught us by human wisdom but in words taught by the Spirit, explaining spiritual realities with Spirit-taught words."[20] States Paul. These are statements of fact and are going to prove highly distasteful to many but that is always the case where the Word is spoken in truth. There is even more provocative scripture to be considered too:- "He said, "Go and tell this people: "Be ever hearing, but never understanding; be ever seeing, but never perceiving." Make the heart of this people calloused; make their ears dull and close their eyes. Otherwise, they might see with their eyes, hear with their ears, understand with their hearts, and turn and be healed."[21] "For this reason they could not believe, "He has blinded their eyes and hardened their hearts, so they can neither see with their eyes, nor understand with their hearts, nor turn and I would heal them."[22] God will blind eyes and harden hearts: "But their minds were made dull, for to this day the same veil remains when the old covenant is read. It has not been removed, because only in Christ is it taken away."[23]

Difficult to cope with? Remember God is motivated only by self-interest, we have dealt with this already; His only objective is to acquire a bride for His son, nothing else is of any consequence to Him, in the end everything else will come to nought, all will be done away with and He will create a new heaven and a new earth in which His Kingdom will absolutely prevail and Jeshua will dwell with His bride. Being omniscient, He is aware of those who will prove to be appropriate candidates for bridehood and those whose who will fall short of the mark. It may be a case of Him 'not casting His pearls before swine'[24] Of course pearls often are cast before swine, but it may be the case that sometimes Father chooses to obstruct the senses of the swine before any pearls can be cast. He is an enigmatic and abstruse God and, again we just have to accept that.

Going back and bearing in mind the discussion on prophesy, the letter, and the Spirit, I am emulating Habakkuk and also writing down what I have been given so that it might be easily read "The revelation awaits an appointed time."[25]. It does not say *what* time, and this may be as good a time as any other, it is almost certainly not the *only* time either! What is also certain is that this word is for today and should be carefully considered and evaluated *in the spirit*! The words do not matter, they killeth! Seek the life! Hereafter, for the rest of chapter 2 God deigns to explain Himself, to a degree, to Habakkuk. No excuses, no accounting, no justification, no elucidation, just a clear statement of one basic fact, of who He is:- "I am that I am!" I am the LORD; that is my name! I will not yield my glory to another or my praise to idols."[26]

I am going directly now to the last verse from Habakkuk. "I give you feet as hinds' feet on high places." This is exactly, word for word, as the Spirit gave it to me- several times. It does not correlate precisely with any of the readily accessible translations but, for the most part, differs only in the odd word or two. Once again, the letter is irrelevant, the Word has been revealed by the Spirit and is absolutely consistent with all legitimate translations. The wording is critical for me, and I would explain why:- "I give you feet as hinds' feet". *I give you;*

I have been given feet as hinds' feet, they have not been earned or striven for nor even desired or coveted; until very recently I had given no thought whatsoever to feet of any sort. Having been given 'feet as hinds' feet is a sovereign act of God, a gift of the Spirit. Feet as hinds' feet *on high places*, I was already inhabiting high places at the end of chapter 13 of this work, I just needed hinds' feet to equip me, properly, for my residency. The thing about having feet as hinds' feet is that the hind is the most sure-footed of creatures. Perfectly happy, safe, and secure even among the most treacherous terrain to be encountered in the high places. Nooks and crannies, precipices, sheer faces and deep gullies, pinnacles and ledges, loose boulders, and disintegrating outcrops; the hind is at home and secure in the midst of them all! The hind does not have to be concerned about her environment, the sense of security and safety is consummate. The mountain lion might be at home up here but even he is no threat; he may, too, be sure-footed in degree but is no match for the hind with regard to agility or speed, she will out-manoeuvre him every time. He will not tarry long if he finds his way up here, there is easier prey to be found on the lower slopes! Having found myself at the end of chapter 13 inhabiting a high place but with no revelation as to what Father's next intent was.

I now know, of course, that His intent was, in His time, to give me feet as hind's feet to equip me for my time of residence in the high places. Apart from the security there are other alluring enchantments to be experienced on the high places. The atmosphere up here is crystal clear; you can see clearly for miles and miles; horizons are expanded, and vistas extended. Most intriguing is the fact that you can see clearly down over and into all the lower slopes and into the valleys below. In spite of the fact that the majority of the ambient hues and textures are white, grey, or marbled there are occasional verdant patches, lush fodder, more than adequate for the sustenance and invigoration of the resident hind; brooks and springs bubble up from unlikely places and refresh with sparkling, living water. Alpines and succulents appear from the most miniscule of cracks and apparently sterile places, they glow with a myriad of tinctures and tones like a vast palette of discovery and revelation. All in all, it is pretty cool, and I am relishing every second!

My version of Habakkuk chapter 3:- "O Lord most Holy and perfect God, you who alone are worthy to be praised, you who are infallible, you who cannot be questioned or challenged, you who speaks and 'it *is*', you who has ordained everything to be worked out in conformity with the purposes of your will, you who are utterly awesome and immaculate; I just acknowledge the fact that you are who you are! I have seen your dealings with men, I do not understand you or them, but I acknowledge your right to act as you see fit. I do not expect any longer to understand your ways in any great depth, I just acknowledge that the highest intelligence of men is absolutely and totally inferior to what might be considered your foolishness.[27] Even if total desolation befalls the earth "yet I will rejoice in the Lord, I will be joyful in God my Saviour. The Sovereign Lord is my strength; he makes my feet like the feet of a deer, he enables me to tread on the heights."[28] All this is not for my benefit, I have no idea why I should be appointed this commission, what I do know is that it is part of my role as a functionary of the Body of Christ. I also know that it will be costly, Jeshua told us "From everyone who has been given much, much will be demanded; and from the one who has been entrusted with much, much more will be asked."[29] I am delighted to testify to the fact that I have been given much and so I am expecting to be asked to share my riches among the gatherings of the Saints. I close with a word for the apostate church:- "Whoever has will be given more; whoever does not have, even what they have will be taken from them."[30]

They tie up heavy burdens and lay them on men's shoulders, but they themselves are unwilling to move them with so much as a finger. "But they do all their deeds to be noticed by men; for they broaden their phylacteries and lengthen the tassels of their garments. "They love the place of honour at banquets and the chief seats in the synagogues, and respectful greetings in the marketplaces, and being called Rabbi by men." Stated Yeshua in Matthew's gospel, chapter 23 verses 5 to 7.

PART 2

A DISCOURSE ON THE DARK NIGHT OF THE SOUL

CHAPTER 15

DOWN TO THE NITTY-GRITTY -
OUT OF THE CRADLE

The remaining chapters of this book have been inspired by a fifteenth century monk. He was imprisoned for a number of years for his' heresies' and would likely have been executed but for the intervention of a significant body of people who had been influenced by his writings. Hence the references to the 'dark night'.

In order to find out what spiritual maturity might entail, it is necessary to understand what spiritual immaturity is, the milk referred to by Peter:- "Like new-born babies, crave pure spiritual milk so that by it you may grow up in your salvation."[1] And by Paul, addressing the Corinthians:- "I gave you milk, not solid food, for you were not yet ready for it. Indeed, you are still not ready."[2] The basic truths of the gospel, regarding original sin and its consequences, God's mercy, repentance, the atoning sacrifice of Christ and the need of faith in Him have greater appeal to the majorities than do the deeper mysteries of the gospel. Men may have much doctrinal knowledge and yet be mere beginners in the life of faith and experience. Arguments about religion have their roots in the flesh. True Christianity makes men peaceable not contentious, but it is sadly true that many who profess to be Christian behave no differently than those who are still in the world. Many self-professing 'men and women of God', fail to exhibit any fruit of the spirit, that is Christlikeness; and instead exhibit carnality, vanity, strife, self-indulgence, self-righteousness, vain-glory, a penchant for dispute, gossip, judgmentalism, and hypocrisy. Note that longevity is not synonymous with maturity!

The journey begins when God, as an act of love and grace, speaks "And the Lord said, "I will cause all my goodness to pass in front of you, and I will proclaim my name, the Lord, in your presence. I will have mercy on whom I will have mercy, and I will have compassion on whom I will have compassion"[3] This is emphasised in the letter to the Romans; and adds "It does not, therefore, depend on human desire or effort, but on God's mercy."[4] So God Himself will lead those who He perceives as appropriate candidates through the night towards the state of epignosis of that divine love which is called agapé, "And to know this love that *surpasses* knowledge that you may be filled to the measure of all the fullness of God."[5] This love is unique to God and the word is hardly used outside of the Newer Testament; it is selfless, all consuming, all embracing, utterly fixated, inexhaustible, incorporeal and immutable love, it might be epitomised as 'other-centred love'. This is absolutely different from another Greek word which is translated in English as 'love' (one of seven), 'philia'; this mainly concerned the deep comradely friendship that developed between brothers in arms who had fought side by side on the battlefield. It was about showing loyalty to friends, sacrificing for them, as well as sharing emotions with them. Storge defined the love between families, parents, and their children. Eros was the sensual component of 'love' which is absent in both agapé and philia. Sadly, it is not until one has entered the dark night that they can escape the confusion that exists between agapé and philia, without epignosis of the former it is impossible to differentiate between them, and without it: "If I speak in the tongues of men or of angels, but do not have love (agapé), I am only a resounding gong or a clanging cymbal."[6]

It is appropriate before going further to discuss some of the characteristics of those who might or might not be called upon by the father to enter into the dark night and to investigate what his motives might be for doing so. It will help those who seek to be weaned and to start to enjoy the 'meatier' piquancy of the spiritual way; to encourage them to accept their condition and take courage and desire that God take them through the experiences which lead to the strengthening of the soul in the pursuit of becoming a true fruit-bearer and experiencing the inestimable delights of agapé. It must be remembered that the one who is genuinely born again and meets the criteria to be discussed will be nurtured by the Father as a mother would nurture her child. This is because the nature of God is without gender, He incorporates both masculinity and femininity[7] So mother will feed the babe on milk from her breast whilst Father holds and supports the infant in His loving arms. However, as the child develops, the mother will start to withhold caresses and to hide her tender love, she will withdraw her support and let the child learn to walk of its own volition until it is weaned from suckling; is able to move on to more cognitive pursuits and grow in agapé and fruit-bearing. This requires no effort on the part of the soul, the grace of God has given the child a passion for things spiritual through the taste and delectation of the milk which has succoured it so far. Because of its tenderness and vulnerability God treats the infant with utmost tenderness and empathy. In this state the soul finds great expression and satisfaction in praise and worship, in prayer, in song and dance, in bible study and discussion of spiritual matters, and all manner of things which it finds satisfying to the soul. Although the spiritually mature also indulge in the same practices, the immature are largely motivated by the consolation and pleasure that they find in them. Because they have not experienced the more demanding aspects of the road to discipleship, there have been no dark nights devoted to seeking the virtues of the truly spiritual person; consequently, their endeavours are not as fruitful as they might be.

To investigate the state of those who might or might not be considered by our Father to be candidates fitted to enter the dark night, we will do well, as best we can, to know the mind of God as he has revealed it to us:- "Who can fathom the Spirit of the Lord, or instruct the Lord as his counselor?"[8] "Who has known the mind of the Lord? Or who has been his counselor?"[9] We can l glean some insights as to what might be an appropriate state of mind; as David proclaimed:- "My sacrifice, O God, is a broken spirit; a broken and contrite heart you, God, will not despise."[10]

This might be a starting point for those who recognise their lack of brokenness and contrition (repentance) and have a desire to have this rectified, on the other hand it would have no relevance for anyone in denial of such needs. "Blessed are those who hunger and thirst for righteousness, for they will be filled."[11] Having a hunger and thirst might also be a prerequisite; this would have to be desperate hunger and a raging thirst, more than could be sated with an iced bun and a latte. Reflecting the sentiment of a psalm of David when he was in the Desert of Judah. "You, God, are my God, earnestly I seek you; I thirst for you, my whole being longs for you, in a dry and parched land where there is no water."[12]

The true believer is convinced, that nothing in this sinful world can satisfy the wants and desires of his immortal soul; he expects his satisfaction to be realised only in being in a state of absolute union with God so far as is attainable in this life. Jeshua posed the question, "Suppose one of you wants to build a tower. Won't you first sit down and estimate the cost to see if you have enough money to complete it?"[13] Preceded by the statement "Whoever does not carry their cross and follow me cannot be my disciple."[14] He also defined the law under which His people had lived for generations with two simple statements, the first and most emphatic of which was:-"Love the Lord your God with all your heart and with all your soul and with all your strength and with all your mind"[15] This demands that before anyone can lay claim to the promises of the Father, that they meet the conditions of the covenant. Most covenants are conditional, a covenant is absolutely binding; it is widely understood that the significance of the two covenantors walking between the two halves of the slain animal is that should either of them break the covenant that they should suffer the same fate. It is vital that the sacrifice and the shedding of blood is not defiled in any way by duplicitous thoughts or intentions; no unspoken 'get out' clauses are incorporated into it; it is absolutely inviolable and sacrosanct. Note that there is a less usual form of covenant in that it is unilateral and unconditional; God made the terms of such a covenant to apply only to Himself, as is the case with the first recorded blood covenant which God made with Abram in Genesis chapter 15, it did not require anything on the part of Abram, so it was unconditional. Compare Leviticus; "*If* you follow my decrees and are careful to obey my commands, I will send you rain in its season, and the ground will yield its crops and the trees their fruit."[16] and "*If* you keep my commands, you will remain in my love, just as I have kept my Father's commands and remain in his love."[17] These are bilateral and conditional covenants, the promise is honoured by the One covenanter (God) if the conditions are met by the other covenanter (us).

This is grossly overlooked by so many who mistakenly think that all of God's promises are there to be partaken of at no cost. Those who are not prepared to pay the price might find themselves ineligible for consideration. Yeshua re-iterated the terms of the covenant: "Not everyone who says to me, 'Lord, Lord,' will enter the kingdom of heaven, but only the one who does the will of my Father who is in heaven."[18] So what might be the hazards of attaching too much virtue to the various practises which appeal so vehemently to the senses, of becoming 'comfortable' with their spiritual life? What are the pitfalls for those who are content to continue to suckle at the breast, who embrace the 'Peter Pan' paradigm, who have no desire or inclination to grow up. Some of the pitfalls of this state will be discussed and how the experiences of the dark night might prove beneficial to those who intend to 'work out their salvation with fear and trembling.'[19]

CHAPTER 16

THE ENCOUNTER WITH OBSTACLE ONE - PRIDE AND PREJUDICE

Consider a babe, who in the course of its first few voyages of discovery outside the cradle, might encounter a footstool which Mum uses to enable her to reach the higher shelves of a bookcase. The babe will recognise it as an obstacle without having any awareness of the functionality of the object; it will not appreciate the fact that this object is both an impediment to progress and an aid simultaneously, this is just one of the many paradoxes to be encountered on the way through the dark night. So it is with the spiritually immature, however "Consider it pure joy, my brothers and sisters, whenever you face trials of many kinds, because you know that the testing of your faith produces perseverance. Let perseverance finish its work so that you may be mature and complete, not lacking anything."[1] It is a small step into the dark night to learn to see God in the midst of everything, "Give thanks in all circumstances; for this is God's will for you in Christ Jesus."[2] and to acknowledge the fact that "In him we were also chosen, having been predestined according to the plan of him who works out everything in conformity with the purpose of his will."[3] The Babes in Christ are fervent in their various religious activities and are inclined to derive pleasure and contentment in the activities themselves. This in itself is not an impediment to progress but what frequently evolves from this is pride! This is a state of satisfaction and contentment with their own works and with themselves, those who are comfortable with their spirituality are going to have to come to terms with the fact that the disciple is never going to be comfortable insofar as his or her state appeals to their senses.

A word about praise and worship here, praise and worship are not what you do, they are a condition of the soul! One aspect of the fruit of the Spirit is humbleness. The flesh and the enemy are adept at mimicking the fruit of the spirit, it is prudent for believers to acquire that feature of the gift of discernment of spirits which is recognising the evidence of pride. We are infested with false teachers and false prophets and probably the most difficult sin for those people to hide is pride; pride, by virtue of what it is, will not subject itself readily to the control of either the one in whom it indwells, *nor the Holy Spirit* and thus is, for the discerning believer, it is reasonably easy to spot. We are told that:- "The person with the Spirit makes judgements about all things, but such a person is not subject to merely human judgements,"[4] That is, if you are a *spiritual person*, you are required to evaluate and assess all things starting, if you are to follow God's order of things, with yourself! To honestly be able to do so one must, with help of the spirit of discernment, be able to judge what is true and what is not. Truth can be categorised as follows: Absolute truth, that which a person has witnessed for themselves or been a party to. It would not matter if such a person were to be taken away and tortured, even unto death, in order to acquire a denial of such a truth, it would remain a truth for eternity. Truth by definition, two plus two equals four; Glasgow is further North than London. Last; truth by consensus; much has been accepted as truth because a number of individuals, not even in many cases, a majority, have decided that a particular statement can be taken as 'true.' Even the scientific community is forever amending, modifying, or even abandoning 'truths.' The earth is the centre of the universe, Christopher Columbus discovered America, the pyramids were built by Hebrew slaves. Even Albert Einstein got some of his theory wrong. "Search me, God, and know my heart; test me and know my anxious thoughts."[5]

From pride comes the desire to speak of spiritual things in the presence of others and even to want to teach them rather than listen and learn. This is Pharisaical pride, puffed up with 'head learning' without any epignosis of what they are talking about. "The Pharisee stood by himself and prayed: 'God, I thank you that I am not like other people- robbers, evildoers, adulterers, or even like this tax collector."[6] The Pharisee who has studied and accumulated a degree of that knowledge which is merely knowledge by consensus and knowledge by definition, neither of which is a substitute for epignosis, he cannot fulfil the role of the true spiritual leader. Let us consider the Words of Yeshua: "Jesus called them together and said, "You know that the rulers of the Gentiles lord it over them, and their high officials exercise authority over them. Not so with you. Instead, whoever wants to become great among you must be your servant."[7] He is establishing the divine order here and making it absolutely clear that there are only two statuses so far as believers are concerned; the head, which is Christ, and we who are the body; as members of the body we have various functions, but all are blessed with the same status, that of servant. There are those who, in the interests of pandering to their sin and love of status and influence would likely quote Hebrews: "Have confidence in your leaders and submit to their authority, because they keep watch over you as those who must give an account. Do this so that their work will be a joy, not a burden, for that would be of no benefit to you."[8]

To quote this without any further consideration and to deny the Word of Christ is at least unwise if not blasphemous and demands some exegesis for the sake of this discourse. 'Leader' in the sense that it is translated from the Greek means 'one who leads the way', one who goes before, one who sets the example *not* one who barks orders and commands from the side as would a vociferous Regimental Sergeant Major evinced by his "don't do what I do- do what I say" approach. To quote further from the Master:- "Whoever wants to be first must be your slave, just as the Son of Man did not come to be served, but to serve, and to give his life as a ransom for many,"[9] and "Jesus said to them, "The kings of the Gentiles lord it over them; and those who exercise authority over them *call themselves* benefactors, but you are not to be like that. Instead, the greatest among you should be like the youngest, and the one who rules like the one who serves."[10] This clearly reveals the mind of Christ on this matter; He is condemning religious overlordship as in one brother having authority over another. The hierarchical authority structure in which there are designated officials in descending order is never embraced nor employed by Jeshua. If your submission to the exclusive authority of another human being is a condition of being accepted into a gathering then you are not enjoying the benefits of the Kingdom, you inhabit the lair of someone else!

This will not lead to disorder but to perfect Holy-Spirit led order; in view of what we have learned regarding the mind of Christ on this matter, it is sensible to peer deeper into this passage from Hebrews. Bearing in mind the edict of Ephesians 5:21:- "Submit to one another out of reverence for Christ."[11] This is an injunction that we should *all* submit to *one another*! The exclusive priesthood has been superseded in Christ, "For it is declared: "You are a priest forever, in the order of Melchizedek."[8] We are all equivalent priests and all of equal status, that is why we are *all* told to submit to one another.[12]

So, what is the point of the writer of Hebrews? Let us consider first what God ordained leadership entails, and how it can be recognised. To start with we should assess and evaluate everything, and with regard to the behaviour of those by whom we are surrounded, the sole criteria to be employed in the evaluation and assessment is 'fruit-bearing'. Jeshua told us "Every tree that does not bear good fruit is cut down and thrown into the fire. Thus, by their fruit you will recognise them. "Not everyone who says to me, 'Lord, Lord,' will enter the kingdom of heaven, but only the one who does the will of my Father who is in heaven."[13] The writer to Hebrews; we can safely assume him, I think, to be approved of God so as to have his writing incorporated into the Scriptures. So let us investigate what he has laid down for the role of 'elder', having first attended to the role of deacon for the sake of clarity. The foundation for the diaconate is found in Acts 6:1-7, the word 'deacon' is not used in the passage but the root word 'diakonia' is, and it describes the role as 'daily administration'; this was used in conjunction with the business of the distribution of food and the waiting on tables. The deacons, as they became known, were appointed to take on a practical role as opposed to the elders whose function was to focus on spiritual matters alone without any encumbrances. Full stop! The scriptural requirements for the roles of deacon and elder make interesting reading, it can be argued that the only significant difference between an elder, or as sometimes translated 'overseer', and a deacon is their function in the Body. The deacons' function was practical and the elders' function spiritual:- "Brothers and sisters, choose seven men from among you who are known to be full of the Spirit and wisdom. We will turn this responsibility over to them and will give our attention to prayer and the ministry of the word."[14] Being full of the Spirit and wisdom are prerequisites for both roles.

In view of what has been said it must be concluded that the writer of Hebrews was aware of the spiritual integrity of the eldership when he wrote his missive, and so he could confidently couch his appeal in the terms in which he did. In view of what was also taught to the Romans:- "So then, each of us will give an account of ourselves to God."[15]; the danger should be highlighted of assuming that the reference to 'those who watch over your souls will give an account'[8] implies that some individuals will have to account for other individuals which justifies their 'lording' it over them. Better to heed the advice of Peter, "Not lording it over those entrusted to you, but being examples to the flock."[16]. Hebrews 13:7 is used to justify religious practices based on fallen human authority structures. "See to it that no one takes you captive through hollow and deceptive philosophy, which depends on human tradition and the elemental spiritual forces of this world rather than on Christ."[17] Advice often ignored.

Inherent in this pride is also the spirit of condemnation, the 'holier than thou' paradigm, self-aggrandisement, and other indicators by which the *spiritual man* can make his evaluations and assessments regarding these folk. Who is it who might inspire and profit from the establishment and the sin of pride in the believer? Satan! He will encourage the growth of pride and presumption in the believer often increasing their fervour and addiction to the satisfaction of the senses, he will encourage the weak and vulnerable in the pursuit of their assumed 'ministries'. He will encourage judgmentalism and censure and he is aware that these activities are just filthy rags in the sight of God because they are designed to appeal to the flesh. Side effects of this pride are distorted vision as observed twice by Yeshua in His dealings with those afflicted: "Why do you look at the speck of sawdust in your brother's eye and pay no attention to the plank in your own eye?"[18] "So you must be careful to do everything they tell you. But do not do what they do, for they do not practice what they preach. They tie up heavy burdens and lay them on men's shoulders, but they themselves are unwilling to move them with so much as a finger. "But they do all their deeds to be noticed by men; for they broaden their phylacteries and lengthen the tassels of their garments. "They love the place of honour at banquets and the chief seats in the synagogues, and respectful greetings in the marketplaces, and being called Rabbi by men."[19] On occasions when those who exhibit the scriptural criteria for eldership endeavour to point out the error of the ways of those that Jeshua was referring to, it is James who offers the truth: "Whoever turns a sinner from the error of their way will save them from death and cover over a multitude of sins."[20] They consider the wise to be unspiritual or lacking in knowledge of spiritual matters, doctrinally flawed or without God-given insight. Consequently, they will desire and contrive to seek the companionability of those who are inclined to encourage and praise their indulgences and pander to their vanity, a subsidiary of pride. These folk are often recognisable by their lust for attention and acknowledgement, not content to be merely used by God for His purposes without desiring any accreditation for themselves. This condition has been emphasised a number of times through scripture:- "Hear this, you foolish and senseless people, who have eyes but do not see, who have ears but do not hear"[21], and "Do you have eyes but fail to see, and ears but fail to hear?"[22] It does well to remember:- "I tell you that to everyone who has, more will be given, but as for the one who has nothing, even what they have will be taken away."[23]

Also symptomatic of this problem is the lack of transparency of the culprit, a reluctance to admit to any personal issues or imperfections, a desire to be regarded as having made some spiritual progress which is not evidenced in their fruit-bearing and a tendency to focus on signs and physical manifestations as presumed indicators of their spiritual standing in lieu of those advocated by Jeshua. They prefer to excuse ungodly conduct of all sorts rather than address the need to have such issues dealt with through the grace of God, the sacrifice of Christ and the ministries of the Holy Spirit. They harbour a deep need to have their devotions, such as they perceive them to be, recognised and appreciated. Remember signs and wonders and the gifts of the Spirit will all pass away, only the fruit will endure through eternity! Sometimes they will become discouraged by their imperfections since their affliction of pride leads them into self-condemnation, so they become impatient and frustrated because they feel themselves to be already qualified as spiritual persons, but not recognising that the ignorant have no means of knowing how far they have yet to go. This in itself contradicts which maintains that "there is now no condemnation for those who are in Christ Jesus"[24]. They often become anxious that God will deal with these imperfections, but their desire is motivated by a longing for a personal peace rather than a closer union with their God. They forget that Father's plan is perfect; "In him we were also chosen, having been predestined according to the plan of him who works out everything in conformity with the purpose of his will."[25] and that "We know that in all things God works for the good of those who love him, who have been called according to his purpose."[26] That the Apostle Paul had to contend with a 'thorn in the flesh' which, it might be supposed, was a particular sin with which he had to constantly battle. Such a proposition is borne out by his confession that "I do not understand what I do. For what I want to do I do not do, but what I hate I do."[27] They do not appreciate that the grace of God extends to the fact that they are allowed to remain in a less than perfect state lest they lapse into greater depths of pride and presumption due to their otherwise improved condition. They are loath to acknowledge genuine spirituality in others but enjoy the attention of others and frequently will expose themselves as attention-seekers.

These infantile tendencies occasionally retrograde into serious error and heretical doctrines. For the majority however, those, the desire of whose hearts is the pursuit of the truth and are beset with a hunger and thirst after righteousness, the grace of God will be sufficient for them. Although none will avoid the pitfalls of infantile fervour which, in itself is a delight to the Father as a baby's first steps are a delight to a human dad; fervour and indulgence have to be managed by those who are walking the way of the dark night and superseded by that aspect of the fruit of the spirit which is humbleness. Humbleness, as stated earlier, is the antonym of pride; they are mutually exclusive, pride and humbleness cannot cohabit, darkness cannot contend with light that is why humbleness is such a significant affirmation of Christlikeness. That is why the discerning disciple will be able to identify pride and self- aggrandisement without difficulty; pride cannot be disguised as humbleness. Those choosing the way of the dark night will be readily recognised by their humbleness, they will be those who pray constantly after the style of David:- "Search me, God, and know my heart; test me and know my anxious thoughts."[28] They have actually died to self and consider themselves to be not of any importance, they are not self-indulgent, they do not need nor desire the recognition and accolades of other men and, as they move on, the more they appreciate the debt they owe to their Saviour and His Father. The greater humility they engender the more the Father will be inclined to employ them in His service for the sake of the fact that they are not inclined to usurp His glory. The more they are employed the less self-satisfied they are, so highly motivated by agapé love are they that they feel that they cannot give enough to Him and shun comparisons with the works of other men.

Accompanying the spiritual assets of humbleness and that state of exquisite contentment which accompanies it, frequently which is called shalom, these souls have a passionate yearning for spiritual knowledge and wisdom. They are aware that such attributes are gifts of the Holy Spirit and that the folly of depending upon human wisdom is to be astutely avoided. They have to have a single-mindedness of purpose:- "If any of you lacks wisdom, you should ask God, who gives generously to all without finding fault, and it will be given to you. But when you ask, you must believe and not doubt, because the one who doubts is like a wave of the sea, blown and tossed by the wind. That person should not expect to receive anything from the Lord. Such a person is double-minded and unstable in all they do."[29] Such folk are the opposite of those identified above, they are not always on the lookout for the naïve and delicate upon whom they can inflict their need for fulfilment as 'teachers'. "But you are not to be called 'Rabbi,' for you have one Teacher, and you are all brothers."[30] stated Jeshua. These embrace a fervent desire to know the truth, not as decreed by scholars and academics but as revealed by the Holy Spirit, the truth is the truth even if no-one believes it to be so, and Jeshua is the truth.[31] There is an inextricable link between humbleness and wisdom and truth as identified by James:- "Who is wise and understanding among you? Let them show it by their good life, by deeds done in the humility that comes from wisdom. But if you harbour bitter envy and selfish ambition in your hearts, do not boast about it or deny the truth. Such "wisdom" does not come down from heaven but is earthly, unspiritual, demonic; for where you have envy and selfish ambition, there you find disorder and every evil practice. But the wisdom that comes from heaven is first of all pure; then peace-loving, considerate, submissive, full of mercy and good fruit, impartial and sincere."[32]

Those who desire to be free of the demon of pride will exhibit the servant heart, they desire to have the mind of Christ; to only do what they see the Father doing;[33,34] They will rejoice in the spiritual progress and edification of others; they have no desire nor need to draw attention to themselves, or their own works as executed under the anointing of the Holy Spirit. "To the only God our Saviour be glory, majesty, power and authority, through Jesus

Christ our Lord, before all ages, now and forevermore!"[35] "To the only wise God be glory forever through Jesus Christ"[36] They will exhibit that spirit which is characterised by purity, genuineness and simplicity which are very pleasing to God. For as the wise spirit of God dwells in these modest folk, He affects them to distract from their perceived achievements and to focus on what still has to be done said Paul:- "One thing I do: forgetting what is behind and straining toward what is ahead"[37] "Do nothing out of selfish ambition or vain conceit. Rather, in humility value others above yourselves,"[38] As Jeshua told us "Do not give dogs what is sacred; do not throw your pearls to pigs. If you do, they may trample them under their feet, and turn and tear you to pieces."[39] "Or do you think Scripture says without reason that *he jealously longs* for the spirit he has caused to dwell in us? But he gives us more grace. That is why it says: "God opposes the proud but shows favour to the humble."[40] Father takes some of us through the dark night in order that we might learn to live the reality of the deeper things of the scriptures.

CHAPTER 17

OF POTENTIAL DIVERSIONS – THE WIDE AND THE NARROW WAY

Many among the immature find themselves fascinated with spiritual things, outside, and as a substitute for the Father, the Saviour, and the Holy Spirit. They become discontent with the truly spiritual and wholly sufficient aspects of the life of the disciple because they do not find what they expect in them. I am talking of the relationships which they would have on a personal, and costly, level with the Godhead. They become dissatisfied, churlish, and petulant, not entirely content with what the spirit God sees fit to bestow upon them. "The Son is the image of the invisible God, the firstborn over all creation. For in him all things were created: things in heaven and on earth, visible and invisible, whether thrones or powers or rulers or authorities; all things have been created through him and for him. He is before all things, and in him all things hold together."[1] From this it may legitimately be inferred that Christ is *only and totally* sufficient. It may be argued that the distractions which are identified and illuminated herein are aspects and evidence of the quality and efficacy of the individual's fellowship and standing in Christ; this may, occasionally, be the case, but more often than not it is an indication of that individual's vulnerability to the distractions described, one of which is defined as parsimony, a tendency to gorge oneself on that which may, or may not, be profitable.

It has always been, and still is, for the members of some cults, to attach themselves to icons, relics, personalities, sites, vestments, idols (both living and inanimate), ideologies and so-on.

They indulge in meetings, DVD's, books, conferences, councils, even Bible study and learning texts and maxims by rote, some have even resorted to physical self-abuse as 'penance'; all instead of seeking the way by which the self may be crucified, and all may be given up in order to qualify as a disciple "If anyone comes to me and does not hate father and mother, wife and children, brothers and sisters, yes, even their own life, such a person cannot be my disciple. And whoever does not carry their cross and follow me cannot be my disciple."[2] "In the same way, those of you who do not give up everything you have cannot be my disciples."[3] The disciple bears an ardent desire to be transformed into a condition of Christlikeness. "Whoever claims to live in him must live as Jesus did."[4] "Who has known the mind of the Lord so as to instruct him?" But we have the mind of Christ."[5] All of these activities, when done in the cause of religiosity or 'doing Christian stuff', are merely substitutes, dummies (otherwise known as comforters) as expiation, often not recognised as such, for wantonness with regard to the edicts and admonitions of Christ in respect of leading the truly spiritual life. There are those who self-indulge in these practices rather than being still and listening for the Word of God to know what His mind is! Regarding these activities as Jeshua did, "Very truly I tell you, the Son can do nothing by himself; he can do only what he sees his Father doing, because whatever the Father does the Son also does."[6] They will rather indulge in some overt religious stuff than be still and just know that He is God. "Be still before the Lord and wait patiently for him; do not fret when people succeed in their ways, when they carry out their wicked schemes."[7]

This is evidence of lack of the fruitfulness that comes from lack of Christ-likeness; part of the fruit of the Spirit is endurance, faithfulness or patience; those who are barren in this area will readily turn to the comfort of the distractions, often in extreme. What is to be condemned, both by those who are truly spiritual and by the Holy Spirit who is the source of all truth. "When he, the Spirit of truth, comes, he will guide you into all the truth. He will not speak on his own; he will speak only what he hears, and he will tell you what is yet to come."[8] The truth is that attachment and affection towards the 'stuff' and the temporary satisfaction that is derived from it are an anathema to the Godhead because they are only, at best, second best. Here is a wonderful and empowering revelation; Praise and worship are not what you do, they are a condition of the soul. "For we maintain that a person is justified by faith apart from the works of the law."[9] That is; we are justified by faith *alone*, not by any works, even those which we claim to be solely expressions of love and joy! Singing, dancing and all sorts of celebration are acceptable only if they are offered in the power of, and under the direction of the Holy Spirit, *not* if they indulged in as an act of conformity or a desire to be seen to be 'super spiritual'. Free to worship in spirit and truth as declared by John: "God is spirit, and his worshippers must worship in the Spirit and in truth"[10] To worship in Spirit and truth transcends rite, tradition, and habit! How many would be seen or heard singing and dancing, lifting up hands or on their knees and faces if they were on their own in private?

Those who are close and attentive to the Spirit will not become attached to visible instruments or burden themselves with them. They do not care to know any more than is necessary to accomplish that which God has set before them because their eyes are fixed on God, on being His friend, and pleasing Him. They yield completely to Him they give all they have; their pleasure is to know how to live for God or neighbour without these religious or temporal things. They are aware that they are doing as the Father does because they are sensitive to the Spirit, hear what He is saying and behave accordingly; they are aware that they have heard the voice of the Father and, thereby have acquired the faith to carry out His demands. As we have been taught; "Faith comes by hearing and hearing by the word of God."[11] Hearing the word of God, as we grow towards maturity, becomes less of a case of looking up a thought for today or a round of 'Pentecostal roulette' (randomly opening a bible and seeing what we can find on the open page) and more a case of 'being still and knowing that He is God'. Until a soul is led by God into the challenges and demands experienced in the dark night it cannot aspire to realise it's potential to be rid of the carnal and sensual. These are the obstacles to the fulfilling of the Father's fervent desire to see us fulfil our maximum potential as imitators of His son to 'do as we see the Father doing.' "Therefore, as dearly loved children walk in the way of love, just as Christ loved us and gave himself up for us as a fragrant offering and sacrifice to God. But among you there must not be even a hint of sexual immorality, or of any kind of impurity, or of greed, because these are improper for God's holy people. Nor should there be obscenity, foolish talk or coarse joking, which are out of place, but rather thanksgiving. For of this you can be sure: No immoral, impure, or greedy person, such a person is an idolater, has any inheritance in the kingdom of Christ and of God. Let no one deceive you with empty words, for because of such things God's wrath comes on those who are disobedient. Therefore, do not be partners with them. For you were once darkness, but now you are light in the Lord. Live as children of light (for the fruit of the light consists in all goodness, righteousness, and truth) and find out what pleases the Lord. Have nothing to do with the fruitless deeds of darkness, but rather expose them. It is shameful even to mention what the disobedient do in secret. But everything exposed by the light becomes visible, and everything that is illuminated becomes a light. This is why it is said: "Wake up, sleeper, rise from the dead, and Christ will shine on you. Be very careful, then, how you live, not as unwise but as wise, making the most of every opportunity, because the days are evil. Therefore, do not be foolish, but understand what the Lord's will is. Do not get drunk on wine, which leads to debauchery. Instead, be filled with the Spirit, speaking to one another with psalms, hymns, and songs from the Spirit. Sing and make music from your heart to the Lord, always giving thanks to God the Father for everything, in the name of our Lord Jesus Christ Submit to one another out of reverence for Chrisr."[12]

This is a reminder to all that the onus is on the individual believer to do their part in the pursuance of the goal of Christlikeness. We took no part in our rebirth, it was an act of grace, but thereafter God expects us to demonstrate and testify to that rebirth by becoming fruit-bearers. The only scriptural indicator of how we shall be known as followers of Christ is by our fruit, "By their fruit you will recognize them. Do people pick grapes from thornbushes, or figs from thistles?"[13] We are required to display a disposition to rid ourselves of all thornbushes and thistles. It is patently clear that we are not able or equipped to effectively overcome every impediment to our achieving Christ-likeness in our own strength but by a demonstration of our determination to do that which we can we might merit the advantage of having the endorsement of God's power, it is this power by which God will free them of those barriers, obstacles and vices which they were unable to overcome by their own efforts. They cannot actively improve their fruit-bearing potential through their own efforts and must rely on the grace of God to do the real refining and cleansing. God must take them through the dark night in order that they might increase His joy and bear much fruit; they will be pruned, the deadwood cut off and removed. "He cuts off every branch in me that bears no fruit, while every branch that does bear fruit he prunes so that it will be even more fruitful."[14] "For, before the harvest, when the blossom is gone and the flower becomes a ripening grape, he will cut off the shoots with pruning knives, and cut down and take away the spreading branches."[15] Those who have yielded all to His service and are totally subject to the Lordship of Christ will find themselves purged in the fire which is the dark night so that they can be brought closer to that state which is as close to perfection and union with divine love as can be achieved whilst still constrained by the flesh. With this in mind "Rejoice always, pray continually, give thanks in all circumstances; for this is God's will for you in Christ Jesus. "Do not quench the Spirit. Do not treat prophecies with contempt but test them all; hold on to what is good, reject every kind of evil. May God himself, the God of peace, sanctify you through and through. May your whole spirit, soul and body be kept blameless at the coming of our Lord Jesus Christ.[16]

It is not the obvious and blatant efforts to persuade a soul to forego self-control, propriety, and chastity but the subtle and sublime assaults made through the senses during moments of devotion and prayer. We must speak here of the matter of meditation and contemplation; they are frequently considered to be interchangeable, however some dictionaries do distinguish between the two as meditation is considered to be the focussing of one's mind, sometimes with the accompaniment of chanting, as a means of relaxation and refreshment. Contemplation, however, is considered to be a state of deep thought with the focus on one problem or enquiry or in a state of planning or in a state of deliberation regarding the making of a decision. They are quite different, and they are so used in many spiritual circles to distinguish between two modes of prayer.

Let us start by using the definition usually employed in such circles. Meditation is a human mode of prayer; it is a steppingstone to contemplative prayer. It is satisfying to those who are young in the faith but is sense-dependent, it will use images, concepts, and reasoning, it will reflect the created order of things and employ those facilities which were created within us and by which we are able to commune with each other and God. It requires human effort to engage and cannot offer other than a remote knowledge of God. It can only be engaged with full understanding; it was the sort of prayer taught by Jeshua to His disciples before He was crucified and before He sent the Holy Spirit. Contemplative prayer is much deeper, the gift of speaking in other tongues is only a steppingstone to the fullness of praying in the spirit, the need to employ the senses is diminished, the understanding and reasoning are redundant, and the soul starts to commune on a higher plane beyond the realms of the flesh and into the unblemished and immaculate realm of the spirit. This is what Paul was expressing in his epistle to the Romans "In the same way, the Spirit helps us in our weakness. We do not know what we ought to pray for, but the Spirit himself intercedes for us through wordless groans. And he who searches our hearts knows the mind of the Spirit, because the Spirit intercedes for God's people in accordance with the will of God."[17] Jeshua told us that we would be given new means of communication over and beyond those with which we had already been blessed; "And these signs will accompany those who believe: In my name they will drive out demons; they will speak in new tongues."[18] There are many believers who will testify that the gift of tongues will mature beyond the articulation of unknown sounds and manifest as crying, groaning and sometimes physical distress. Such experiences were patently familiar to Paul, that is why he refers to 'wordless groans and stresses that 'the Spirit intercedes for God's people *in accordance with the will of God*'. This reflects Jeshua's own practice:- "Very truly I tell you, the Son can do nothing by himself; he can do only what he sees his Father doing, because whatever the Father does the Son also does."[19]

The object of the passage through the dark night is to allow God to help us dispense with our reliance on the senses insofar as they are a means to a deeper and more intense relationship with our creator. Many are self-satisfied with their relationship not realising or appreciating that our Father desires, even hungers for; something ever deeper and more fulfilling for both the creator and the created. For those whose *hunger and thirst after righteousness* are paramount! He will offer them an intensity of spiritual life beyond that which they can think or ask, He only asks that they submit to His dealing with those worldly parts of us which have not been put to death in the course of the re-birth. His passion is that we should submit to His desire to make us into the likeness of His son. Failure to submit can have serious consequences. Even those who call Him Lord but are not willing to submit are in mortal danger, as Jeshua has warned us that "Not everyone who says to me, 'Lord, Lord,' will enter the kingdom of heaven, but only the one who does the will of my Father who is in heaven."[20]

The focus of this section is to make aware to those who are experiencing the dark night of the diversions that may be offered even when one is engaged in contemplative prayer. Whether described as 'lust' or 'luxury' they are impure feelings and thoughts which arise beyond the candidate's control and have one of three roots. The first are an effect of the pleasure derived from human nature in the performance of spiritual exercises. Since the spirit and the senses both take pleasure in the practices, each take delight according to its own nature and inclinations. The Spirit, the incumbent constituent of the soul, imbibes the more refined and uncontaminated union with God. The senses, the lower and carnal part of the soul feel some degree of satisfaction and fulfilment because it believes that there is nothing which is superior and will grasp at whatever is procurable in the belief that it is the ultimate state. Often, in the midst of fervent prayer and devotion, thoughts, images, reflections, nostalgia, and various other sense-based and almost certainly pleasurable diversions will overwhelm and divert the pray-er from his/her intended purpose. The sensory part of the soul is less than perfect; it where darkness dwells, it is where lust, greed, covetousness, pride, vanity, intolerance, and a multitude of other vices all dwell. God's Spirit is contaminated by but not excluded by this profusion of vice but will work, with the collaboration of the individual, to lead that person through the purgative experience of the dark night so that these maladies might be dealt with, and healing administered. This state is not entirely satisfactory so far as the Father is concerned, "For what do righteousness and wickedness have in common? Or what fellowship can light have with darkness?"[21] It will then be the spiritual part of the soul, rather than the carnal which becomes ultra-sensitised to the moving of God's spirit; thus the soul receives everything according to the mode of the spirit. This enabled Paul to state "Who has known the mind of the Lord so as to instruct him? But we have the mind of Christ."[22] and "My conscience is clear, but that does not make me innocent. It is the Lord who judges me."

The second source of these diversions is the devil, in order to divert the saint from his intentions he will try to introduce distractions of the sensual sort. They are often of a sexual nature but frequently he uses other attractions as bait, the very personal circumstance being exploited, especially if one is in the throes of the dark night experience. Worldly ambitions are another favourite, especially the lust for religious status, the immature lacking humbleness are particularly vulnerable. Frequently the distractions are tainted with the flavour of pseudo-spirituality, they are designed to appear as if they are affairs ordained by God to be given special meditation. This is contrary to His purpose in taking us through the dark night as we know now that meditation is only a transient state for those who are taking the road of the contemplative; Satan would sooner distract you from this path if he is unable to completely divert you from your purpose.

The third source of distraction is the fear of distraction itself, something of the flesh might be sufficient to refresh a remembrance of an occasion when one suffered a feeling of abject failure at having been distracted in their devotions to the extent that they were rendered incapable of resumption due to all thoughts of their activities having been excluded and forgotten. "For God has not given us a spirit of fear and timidity, but of power, love, and self-discipline."[23] This will be evident in the mature believer but those who are still in the throes of the purging grace will still be susceptible to apprehension and timidity, fear of failure and inadequacy, of impotence; and vulnerability will gain footholds and influence. Grief and melancholy are most potent when employed in the manner described, the self-discipline aspect of the spiritual fruit is most fragile at such times.

Sometimes again, especially when carrying out spiritual activities, persons are inclined to be overcome with vigour and immodesty with regard to the others who might be witness to their various activities, these are symptoms of an insidious and rarely discerned spirit. This is the smug spirit otherwise discerned as the spirit of spiritual lust. It is closely related to the spirits of pride, arrogance, self-aggrandisement, and self-gratification.

'Self' is the door by which carnal love can become a significant distraction. Carnal love is defined in the original language of the Newer Testament as philia. Philia is the love as experienced in the senses, the very closest of bonds between humans. It also embraces the bonds between groups or individuals who have common experiences either traumatic or exhilarating such as brothers at arms or pioneers. Most dominant are those between family members, storge in the Greek, both blood relatives and those related by marriage Another word translated into English as 'love' is agapé, this is distinct and alien to philia as it is applied only to God. It is love devoid of sensuality, others centred, unwavering and exquisite in every sense. God, however, does not belittle philia in any way, in fact He encourages it throughout scripture. However, the conflict of interests generated by the two is problematical for the believer intent on pursuing the deeper spiritual life. Because the senses and the spirit are essentially incompatible, one love will tend to grow at the expense of the other, as Jeshua said:- "Flesh gives birth to flesh, but the Spirit gives birth to spirit."[24]. That is that which has its origin in the senses will end in the senses and that which is of the spirit ends in God and produces growth. He who hungers and thirsts after righteousness will have to acknowledge these truths when he enters the dark night and submit to the establishment of these loves in reasonable order. The night brings these under control and puts them in proper order, it strengthens and purifies the love, which is of God and, comparatively speaking, diminishes the other.

CHAPTER 18

THE DAWNING OF DUSK

A good way to start a chapter I thought; might an oxymoron provoke a bit more interest? However, there is more to it than that. As the dawn is the slow and inevitable impingement of light into darkness so dusk is the slow withdrawal of that light and the restricting of the functionality of the senses. Our discourse moves on now to the investigation proper into the dark night, its implications, its phenomena, and its various manifestations. This dark night, described as contemplation, is designed to purge the two aspects of the soul, the sensual and the spiritual; one night is focused on the purging of the sensual and the other night by which the spirit is purged and rendered broken and contrite as declared by David "My sacrifice, O God, is a broken spirit; a broken and contrite heart you, God, will not despise."[1] The broken and contrite spirit is the spirit prepared for union with God through agapé, so far as is possible whilst constrained within the human body. The sensory night is not uncommon and is experienced in varying degrees by many, and it is of this night to which the discourse will be first directed. The second night is the portion of the very few, devised for those whom Father recognises as those who qualify as disciples, genuinely hunger and thirst after righteousness, and have endured the purging of the senses and the infilling of the Holy Spirit into the territories hitherto occupied by the flesh, and the exposed and susceptible areas of the mind.

Testimonies of those who have traversed the dark night are few, and the notion that God subjects His children to such probation is an anathema to many so-called believers. This is blatantly contrary to scripture and a lie propagated by false teachers which is ingested by those whose ears are itching. "For the time will come when people will not put up with sound doctrine. Instead, to suit their own desires, they will gather around them a great number of teachers to say what their itching ears want to hear."[2] For those who love the truth, such lies are clearly disproved:- "We also glory in our sufferings, because we know that suffering produces, perseverance, character, and character hope[3] "Consider it (the Dawning of Dusk) to be pure joy my brothers and sisters whenever you face trials of many kinds, because you know that the testing of your faith produces perseverance. Let perseverance finish its work so that you may be mature and complete, not lacking anything."[4]

Since, as discussed, the conduct of these babes is immature and focused on sense and self, and it is the Father's desire to liberate them from this lower state, and to elevate them to a higher plane of agapé and union. He starts to do this when the babes have become turgid and unsated with milk and have started to grasp the reality of the deeper states of the soul and to recognise that the aridity which they are starting to experience is the way by which they shall find the true refreshment they seek. The book of Job, whose own experience of the dark night is the embodiment of the whole matter, is a source of insight into what God teaches us in these circumstances. Elihu's words in Job are to be noted:- "People cry out under a load of oppression; they plead for relief from the arm of the powerful. But no one says, 'Where is God my Maker, who gives songs in the night, who teaches us more than he teaches the beasts of the earth and makes us wiser than the birds in the sky?" Under trial and tribulation and aridity the people cry out, they plead for relief; but, says Elihu, they fail to cry out to God[5]. This is patently not the case for the believer who recognises the validity of the dark night and who, as demonstrated in verse 11, acknowledges that apart from giving us songs in the night, that is endurance and perseverance, He imparts learning and wisdom. It is in the tribulation that the power and strength of the gospel and the believer are exemplified; if God is to give us songs in the night, He must first make the night. In the darkness they will experience the Word:- "I know your deeds. See, I have placed before you an open door that no one can shut. I know that you have little strength, yet you have kept my word and have not denied my name."[6] In the darkness they find no solace in their old meditative activities, in this dry state they can derive no satisfaction and pleasure from exercises and works and may even find them distasteful. When the Father sees that they are starting to grow He weans them from the breast, leaves off their nappies and sets them down to grow accustomed to walking unaided. Those whose laying down of their life in the course of their rebirth has been more thorough will likely begin to enter the dark night much earlier than those whose commitment to the new life is curtailed by vestiges of worldliness. For those who still question the validity of the dark night, the purging experience is to be testified to throughout the whole of scripture both individually and corporately.

Since it may be the case that the symptoms of having entered the dark night might not be distinguishable from the same as those experienced by those who blatantly continue to sin, who are weak and lukewarm, or who suffer physical or mental illness; it will be profitable to understand how one can ascertain the source of his or her trial. Firstly, it will be apparent that the candidate experiencing the dark night will not only find no sensual satisfaction in his or her religious activities but will find none in their corporeal activities either. Since God's purpose in this time of aridity is to purge the sensory appetite, He allows no satisfaction in the indulgence of anything which might satisfy any of these appetites. However, since the lack of satisfaction in anything could be due to depression or other mental or physical illness a second indicator is seemly. The second is the fact that those who are undergoing the purging of the senses will recall with some unease their various devotions and exercises; they will feel that their lack of enthusiasm for things religious is a failure to serve God and may become melancholic. If this state is the effect of back-sliding, apostasy, or wilful sin, then there will be no sense of deprivation and dispossession as experienced by those who are undergoing the purging of those appetites which are an impediment to the reaching of the high places to be found only in God. The reason for this dryness is that in order to bear the fruit of the spirit, which is Christ-likeness, the soul must be refreshed solely by that living water as described by Jeremiah:-"My people have committed two sins: They have forsaken me, the spring of living water, and have dug their own cisterns, broken cisterns that cannot hold water."[7], and from John:-"Jesus answered her, "If you knew the gift of God and who it is that asks you for a drink, you would have asked him and he would have given you living water."[8] It is through this living water that God transfers His gifts which lead to fruitfulness and authority from strength to spirit; since the sensory part of the soul is not fitted to receive and drink of this living water it remains unnourished and parched. Meanwhile the spirit becomes refreshed, edified, and informed, it is in these times that one is likely to start receiving legitimate revelations from their Father. They will become more alert and sensitive, more solicitous in their attention to their *spiritual* duties and have travelled further up the mountain towards the high places as described thus: -"The Sovereign Lord is my strength; he makes my feet like the feet of a deer, he enables me to tread on the heights."[9]

Those whom God leads into these wilderness experiences are akin to those experienced by the children of Israel:- "The rabble with them began to crave other food, and again the Israelites started bewailing the Dawning of Dusk and said, "If only we had meat to eat! We remember the fish we ate in Egypt at no cost- also the cucumbers, melons, leeks, onions, and garlic. But now we have lost our appetite; we never see anything but this manna!"[10] If those who, in the midst of these trials, heed the word of God and follow His precepts "He says, Be still, and know that I am God; I will be exalted among the nations, I will be exalted in the earth."[11] "But they that wait upon the Lord shall renew their strength; they shall mount up with wings as eagles; they shall run, and not be weary; and they shall walk, and not faint."[12] They will soon learn that in their times of inactivity, quiet and focus they will find the refreshment that comes from the living water and they will learn that this refreshment and infilling of the Spirit does not come from the striving or desire of it for it is this degree of contemplation, as defined earlier, that is active when the soul is in repose and undistracted; it is like air which escapes as one tries to grasp it! It is in this state that the realisation that a desire to work with the faculties would be detrimental to spiritual growth rather than an asset, whereas in the novice years of the spiritual life the converse was the case. In the contemplative state it is God who works in it free from the encumbrances of corporeality. It is in this state that the contemplative will experience and delight in that Godly peace which is described as 'shalom', a condition which I describe as 'exquisite contentment'. That is not just an absence of hostilities, that which is generally regarded by most people as a state of peace; but something much broader and enriching. It is exquisite contentment and completeness, wholeness, joy, relief and a sense of vindication, overall, a sense of fruitfulness acquired without effort.

The third sign is the sense of powerlessness, the inability to find communion with God through the senses as one did earlier; in spite of all striving and human endeavour the aridity remains. God does not any more communicate through the senses, through words and ideas and imaginings but communicates through pure spirit transcending words and thoughts. This is described by Paul in his letter to the Romans "In the same way, the Spirit helps us in our weakness. We do not know what we ought to pray for, but the Spirit himself intercedes for us through wordless groans."[13] From this time on the soul will fail to find the degree of satisfaction that it did in its meditative state as it did earlier, it will be less sure of its efficacy with regard to prayer as it did. Were this state to be the effect of any condition other than the passage into the dark night then it would be possible, with some effort, to re-establish their old habits and patterns. For those moving onward and upward it is not possible because having entered the state of powerlessness, which is a manifestation of complete humbleness and submission, one can only be further absorbed into it. Of course, it is not likely that anyone will be totally deprived of the ability and opportunity to resort to the meditative state where they can resort to the employment of the senses, but it is likely, if their desires for advancement are to be met, that they will be more inclined to leave such retrograde activities further and further behind.

All true believers will harbour a deep desire for spiritual gratification, for those who still crave milk this will be sated by the indulgence in spiritual activities which appeal to the flesh. However, when these delights are over and the activity ceases, these infants will often feel unsatisfied or depleted at the lack of exercise and become susceptible to frustration or peevishness. Without any bolstering of the spirit through sensual means they will be inclined often to nostalgic reflection and wishful thinking, this is contrary to the mandate: "Rejoice always; pray without ceasing; in everything give thanks; for this is God's will for you in Christ Jesus. Do not quench the Spirit; do not despise prophetic utterances but examine everything carefully; *hold* fast to that which is good and abstain from every form of evil."[14] Once the elation and exhilaration have waned, they are like a child who has tasted sweet breast milk and crave more of the same. This is not ungodly or worldly, but it *is* fleshy and an impediment to growth which can only be purged in the dark night.

The same applies to those who are seduced into a state of frustration or even anger over the imperfections of others. Those who indulge in pride and arrogance, who set themselves up as paragons of virtue and become intolerant or disdaining of those who, in their opinion, lack the maturity and spirituality which they perceive to be evident in themselves. All these imperfections belie any semblance of Christlikeness and certainly invalidate any assertions of being led and guided by the Holy Spirit. Likewise, they establish a propensity to bear thistles and thorns rather than the fruit of the spirit. Anger is the antithesis of gentleness and kindness; frustration the antithesis of long-suffering and patience and all of them contrary to the ideal of meekness and humbleness. Impatience is the manifestation of the ignorance of those who are ignorant of, or choose to ignore, the way God works in dealing with humanity. Those who have any depth of understanding of His ways will know that His timing is not subject to the desires of man; "But do not forget this one thing, dear friends: With the Lord a day is like a thousand years, and a thousand years are like a day."[15] "There is a time for everything, and a season for every activity under the heavens"[16]. "Jeshua said to them: "It is not for you to know the times or dates the Father has set by his own authority."[17] It is evident that God having, as we have seen, ordained everything to be worked out in conformity with the purposes of His will that His plan and, therefore, His timing is perfect. To be reduced to frustration, anger or any sort of discontentment is a statement of conflict with His perfect condition and is an anathema to Him. It is relevant for the believer of any degree to realise that anything which causes him/her to be robbed of their state of shalom, such as the vices under discussion, is contrary to Fathers' desire and plan for us. It is an aspect of the fruit of the spirit and a requirement for the disciple who desires to bear fruit for the benefit of others (which is the sole role of the fruit-bearer). "Peacemakers who sow in peace reap a harvest of righteousness."[18]

This part of the experience has been described as spiritual gluttony, it must be said that for the modern reader this might not be the most explicative heading for this section as, for the modern reader, gluttony will readily be read as greed, avarice or covetousness. However spiritual gluttony goes beyond the realms of the usual contexts in which the word is used and ensnares many of those whose delight is still contained within their religious practices and indulgences. Many still savour the spiritual satisfaction which has been enjoyed hitherto through such indulgence and crave more of the same rather than spiritual purity and discretion; yet it is this purity and discretion that God earnestly desires and finds acceptable.

It is written that:- "My sacrifice, O God, is a broken spirit; a broken and contrite heart you, God, will not despise." King David writes this whilst in the throes of undergoing the dark night of the soul; he continues to share his revelation of what God is teaching him within this statement:- "You do not delight in sacrifice, or I would bring it; you do not take pleasure in burnt offerings."[19] This is a far cry from his earlier inclinations:- "David built an altar to the Lord there and sacrificed burnt offerings and fellowship offerings. Then the Lord answered his prayer on behalf of the land, and the plague on Israel was stopped."[20] This is one of many testimonies to be found in scripture of the maturing of the individual, the purging of the sensually attractive and the supplementing with the deeper things of the purer spiritual union with God. Followed by one of the most beautiful and revealing of all scriptures, the assertion that, by the grace of God, a human has been able to experience one of the fundamental truths of the spiritual life." My sacrifice, O God, is a broken spirit; a broken and contrite heart you, God, will not despise."[21] This is the only sacrifice totally acceptable to God; all else, including sacrifices involving works or effort, are inferior although, for the sake of weaker and less mature believers, God will honour such, especially when endorsed by one who is in the better place. "May it please you to prosper Zion, to build up the walls of Jerusalem. Then you will delight in the sacrifices of the righteous, in burnt offerings offered whole; then bulls will be offered on your altar."[22] So says King David.

Unable to offer anything more patently sinful with any prospect of success, satan will frequently stir up this gluttony in the believer; so, they become even more indulgent in their pursuit of what they consider to be spiritually satisfying Bigger and more elaborate venues, louder and more widely publicised bands, world-famous speakers, impressive bookshelves, DVD collections and the like are all employed to keep the target from moving on to the more enduring and dynamic virtues of the Holy Spirit. Not that these diversions in themselves are sinful or even unprofitable for spiritual people, indeed we know, hopefully, that God uses everything to the good of His children and that many are edified and strengthened through these resources. However, satan would rather them remain impotent and ignorant as they are in their existing condition than progress and become more enabled to be genuine fruit-bearers. He will persuade them to continue in their semi-enlightened state and continue to act as they are inclined to do rather than be led of the Spirit. As Jeshua advocated by example when sharing with His disciples:- "Very truly I tell you, the Son can do nothing by himself; he can do only what he sees his Father doing, because whatever the Father does the Son also does."[23]

Some will experience some of the aspects of the dark night and start to find less and less satisfaction in their usual religious pursuits and display the sinful traits which become evident as frustration and testiness, they become less tolerant and discouraged, they think that because they are not indulging in the sensual that they are not serving God. They think that gratifying and satisfying themselves is serving and satisfying God. They will not recognise, at least at first, that the aridity and sense of wilderness are part of God's strategy for freeing the infant from the reliance and palatability of milk. The dark night incorporates the wilderness experience, that time of trial and testing, of proving and qualifying so frequently documented in the scriptures that God uses to cause His people to increase in character and stature, and to acquire a greater understanding of Himself and His ways. One of these episodes is adopted by Jeremiah when remonstrating with Israel over their conduct and lack of spirituality: - "They did not ask, 'Where is the Lord, who brought us up out of Egypt and led us through the barren wilderness, through a land of deserts and ravines, a land of drought and utter darkness, a land where no one travels and no one lives?"[24] It is to be noted that it was *the Lord* who led them through the dark night and also remembered that in the early days of their sojourn they revealed their ungracious nature and their sin of gluttony:-"The Israelites said to them (Moses and Aaron), "If only we had died by the Lord's hand in Egypt! There we sat around pots of meat and ate all the food we wanted, but you have brought us out into this desert to starve this entire assembly to death."[25] This episode also reveals part of God's purposes here: - "Then the Lord said to Moses, "I will rain down bread from heaven for you. The people are to go out each day and gather enough for that day. In this way *I will test them* and see whether they will follow my instructions."[26]

Those who succumb to such gluttony will lose, or have lost, sight of the depths out of which they have been raised or the heights to which they have been called. Thorns and thistles will manifest themselves as lack of humbleness, pride in works, and failure to accredit God with all the glory. For them, impatience, apathy, and unreliability rule. They mistrust of themselves that they might please God alone without all the razzmatazz and effort, they are unable to heed the exhortation to "Be still before the Lord and wait patiently for him; Do not fret when people succeed in their ways, when they carry out their wicked schemes.[27] Because they have lost sight of the depths and heights involved in their salvation, they also lose sight of the conditions of the way of the cross. "Then he called the crowd to him along with his disciples and said: "Whoever wants to be my disciple must deny themselves and take up their cross and follow me. For whoever wants to save their life will lose it, but whoever loses their life for me and for the gospel will save it."[28] Way before the time of Christ, following years of disobedience and retribution, the Israelites still experienced the grace of their God. He had sent Ezra, the prophet who had brought the Law of Moses back to them, which had a profound effect, even reducing them to tears of remorse. He had told them: - "Go, eat of the fat, drink of the sweet, and send portions to him who has nothing prepared; for this day is holy to our Lord. Do not be grieved, for the joy of the Lord is your strength. So the Levites calmed all the people, saying, "Be still, for the day is holy; do not be grieved." All the people went away to eat, to drink, to send portions and to celebrate a great festival, because they understood the words which had been made known to them."[29]

Only when we have the full realisation of His awesome majesty and our own unconscionable state outside of Christ can we enter that state of exquisite joy which is our strength. It is this 'joy unspeakable' which is part of the fruit of the spirit discussed earlier. It sustains us throughout the journey and is brought to ultimate fruition in this life when our light is so strong that it violates the darkness and enables the disciple to fulfil his or her commission to spend on behalf of the hungry and satisfy the needs of the oppressed.

CHAPTER 19

A FEW ENCOURAGING
GLINTS OF SONLIGHT –
THE TWO-EDGED SWORD

This is the state at which the ancient monk declares the start of the second phase of the dark night, that which deals with the spirit having sufficiently dealt with the senses. He emphasises that the transition will not be immediate but will be time-consuming and will last for a long time after having left the state of the suckling babe and shed, so far as is possible, the addictions to things sensual. He likens it to one who has been liberated from a horrific imprisonment, the adjustment will, of necessity, take a great deal of time. Having not previously experienced the liberty, the pilgrim will only be able to assimilate and ingest the newly acquired delights of agapé, shalom and joy unspeakable at an appropriate rate lest he or she suffer from acute spiritual dyspepsia. The beneficiary will experience greatly heightened sensitivity to these delights by virtue of having benefited from the times of aridity and famine, and this fact will demand some deal of time for the purpose of acclimatisation. It is during this time that more times of aridity and famine will be experienced, and these will be even darker than previously, but they will serve to emphasise the brightness of the new experiences as described earlier.

It is essential, now, to acquire an understanding of what, according to scripture, defines the soul. I acknowledge, before I start, that my main sources, as I have been directed to by the Holy Spirit, are all globally recognised as exegetes of exceptional understanding and reputation. They would all be recognised as such by most believers. Sadly, the majority are deceased, so that might not apply to those who are young and might not be, yet, widely read. I am aware, from the preface of one of my source books, that these prophets, for that is what they are, having all experienced the dark night of the spirit themselves and learnt from it, would not want any degree of acknowledgement or accreditation. Their sources are scripture backed up by epignosis; their source, as is mine, is the Holy Spirit and He will not allow us to appropriate any part of the glory which is due to our living God.

"May God himself, the God of peace, sanctify you through and through. May your whole spirit, soul and body be kept blameless at the coming of our Lord Jesus Christ."[1] Note that three facets of the human condition are stated: - spirit, soul, and body. This is not to be read as whole: - spirit soul and body! Soul is *not* synonymous with body. This is proven in scripture explicitly: - "For the Word of God is alive and active. Sharper than any double-edged sword, it penetrates even to dividing soul and spirit, joints, and marrow; it judges the thoughts and attitudes of the heart."[2] Note that the Word of God divides; this is what we were warned of by Jeshua, in Luke "Do you think I came to bring peace on earth? No, I tell you, but division."[3] Before we discuss the division and the separation, which was the subject of the second part of the 'dark night', let us investigate what the distinctions are between these three facets of our being. This needs to be done in reverse order, not for reasons of anything other than relevance and chronology.

Back to the beginning: - "Then the Lord God formed a man from the dust of the ground and breathed into his nostrils the breath of life, and the man became a living being."[4] First, God formed man(kind) from the dust of the ground, *then* He breathed life into him. This inanimate pile of dust, or clay, became a human being; Jeshua told us that: - "The Spirit gives life; the flesh counts for nothing. The words I have spoken to you-, they are full of the Spirit and life."[5] The 'life' in the man was due to God having breathed into him 'spirit'. The flesh, that which had been formed from what God had already created counts for nothing; only when it had been empowered with spirit did it become what we would call a cognitive being. The 'flesh' (dust, mud, clay) and the spirit amalgamated to become a person, this amalgamation of flesh and spirit became a 'soul'. Note that this spirit is not the same as the Holy Spirit but only that aspect of it which gives 'life'! How do we know this? Because "The Spirit himself testifies with our spirit that we are God's children."[6] and "The Spirit of God has made me; the breath of the Almighty gives me life."[7] The spirit referred to above as 'our spirit' is the spirit of man as declared by Zechariah:- "The Lord, who stretches out the heavens, who lays the foundation of the earth, and who forms the human spirit within a person."[8] This *not* the same as the Holy Spirit. The spirit, as appertains to man, is discussed hundreds of times in the scriptures, it is also another element in the 'being made in the likeness of God' since He is wholly Spirit; and is of greatest value in considering the condition of the soul. Note that throughout scripture, as translated into English, defines God's Spirit with a capital 'S', and mankind's spirit with a lower case 's'. This miraculous fact might be likened to having flour and water which when combined form dough; the dough is the soul, the amalgam of flesh and spirit. Now we see why, in the letter to the Thessalonians, Paul refers to us as "spirit, soul and body", in that order. Because, in the proper order of things, the spiritual is paramount, but the flesh is condemned to return from whence it came, and the soul is?? Well, it is certainly that part of us which has the potential for everlasting life as Jeshua told us:- "Do not be afraid of those who kill the body but cannot kill the soul. Rather, be afraid of the one who can destroy both soul and body in hell."[9] and "For God so loved the world that he gave his one and only Son, that whoever believes in him shall not perish but have eternal life."[10] The 'dough', referred to earlier, can be of varying consistencies, more water makes it more pliable, more flour, less pliable; more under the influence of the flour (flesh) or more under the influence of the water (spirit)? So, we can see that the soul can be influenced one way or the other by either the flesh or the spirit. To further make the distinction; it is the flesh which gives us world-consciousness through the senses, the spirit gives God-consciousness because we owe our very life-breath to Him, and our soul gives us self-consciousness. It is because we have this spiritual facet of our soul that everyone finds a need for some sort of spiritual satisfaction which has led to a predisposition towards all sorts of forms of religiosity and idolatry. Many will claim that they have no such predisposition, but they deceive themselves. "The prudent understand where they are going, but fools deceive themselves."[11] These people all worship something or *someone*, often themselves. The soul is cognitive and sentient, that is it has self-consciousness, it is aware of its existence, it has consciousness and the power of perception through the senses. It has the facilities of perception, memory, reasoning, and judgement. The soul is the unique personality of the individual; the intellect, the emotions and the *will* are all therein.

The emphasis is on the will because this is the most crucial and far-reaching aspect of our soulish condition. Back to Genesis again:- "Then God said, "Let us make mankind in our image, in our likeness, so that they may rule over the fish in the sea and the birds in the sky, over the livestock and all the wild animals, and over all the creatures that move along the ground."[12] There is a vast amount of verbiage disseminated regarding Genesis 1:26; many questions are posed and few of them answered categorically. One of them has been concerning gender, according to the next verse, "male and female He created them." This poses the question:- "what does 'having been made in God's image; in His 'likeness' actually mean for us?" One aspect of having been made in 'His likeness' which we can all identify with, is that we have been made with a 'will' which is now, and always has been, an active and integral component of the soul. What gender(s), if any, God might have exhibited at the creation are irrelevant. Knowing the paradoxical nature of our God I would suggest neither *and* both, as He is totally Spirit, there is no way He could incorporate any genitalia in His 'image'. What is indisputable is that He omnipotent and can do, and does, whatsoever He pleases, this is free-will and the most significant attribute that was passed on to humanity in Adam. We also know from scripture, which has been discussed before, that God cannot lie, He *is* truth, and He cannot break a covenant if its conditions are met. This does not affect His free-will because this is what He *is*, not what He is able to decide, it is integral to His being. So, in his original state, Adam could not do so either.

It would seem likely that Adam would also have had other attributes pertaining to having been made in the image and likeness of God. These would have included supernatural powers which enabled him to communicate effectively with the spirit world, thus he was able to converse with satan. Later, this power, which had become latent after the fall, was used to communicate with the spirit world as in the case of Saul's summoning of Samuel's spirit by the witch at Endor.[13] This is still common practice in spiritualism and many Eastern religions. It was likely that Adam would have also possessed extraordinary powers in other areas, physique, and intellect among them; these are still latent in every person, but some are able to find access to them by various practices and account for many of the phenomena witnessed by people practising religions not related to the God of Abraham, Isaac and Jacob and to Jeshua, His Son.

"Do you not know that you are God's temple and that God's Spirit dwells in you?"[14] The temple is divided into three distinct areas; the outer court, the inner court, and the inner sanctum. Man's soul, his temple, is also of three areas as has been discussed; his body is like the outer court, which is the outermost part of his being, and can be observed and inspected by all and sundry, it is one of the influences on the soul, the one which makes the constant demands via the senses and the one which had to be dealt with first in the passage of the dark night. This is the part which is destined to return into the earth and have no more part to play. Of course, the one exception is Jeshua, the perfect and uncorrupted man. The inner sanctum is the sacred place where man's spirit dwells, it can only be entered if the veil of his heart has been rent asunder in the process of regeneration, having been born again. The inner court is the soul, the area in which the outer court and the inner sanctum are connected, and all are contained within the one composition which is the temple.

At the fall, in the garden of Eden, whilst Adam was still spiritually astute and still familiar with all things spiritual, he violated his God-likeness by the fact that he breached his covenant with his creator. Remember that God had handed over the 'whole earth' to Adam,[15] this was a covenant. It is not a 'blood covenant' but a covenant nonetheless; Adam made no statement indicating his declining of the offer, thus he had tacitly agreed to the only conditional part of the covenant: - "You must not eat from the tree of the knowledge of good and evil, for when you eat from it you will certainly die."[16] Because, as has already been pointed out, Adam inherited his free-will from his creator along with other attributes, and he was aware of this fact, now being sentient. Although, one wonders, if Adam had any real concept of what death might involve. But God could not have made the situation any easier for Adam and Eve, only one tree was excluded, they had every other plant on the planet at their disposal, including the tree of life right beside the forbidden one, which has been the redemption for us through Christ.

What was the point of all this? The answer is in the fact that man had been created with free-will. One is only able to exercise free-will if one has an opportunity to abuse it, otherwise he would just be an automaton, absolutely incapable of exercising free-will. We know that we need to demonstrate our love of our Father and He has told us how we must fulfil that requirement, "If you love me, keep my commands."[17] We now understand that God gave Adam just one command to enable him to demonstrate his love, but he blew it! If he had not free-will he would have been unable to demonstrate his love of God. As it happens, we wonder if Adam had to fall. Perhaps if you are created in the likeness of God, you already had agapé love, but that would be outside the scope of your free-will because it would not be a matter of choice if the decision had already been made for you. Paradoxically perhaps agapé is not entirely compatible with the unregenerate man. Perhaps it is only a fallen man who has been redeemed by the sacrifice of Christ who can be moved to such an intensity of love as is agapé.

To resume our considerations of the soul we shall discuss the spiritual aspect of it since it is this part which the original manuscript addresses now. "For the word of God is alive and active. Sharper than any double-edged sword, it penetrates even to dividing soul and spirit, joints and marrow; it judges the thoughts and attitudes of the heart."[18] Since we have now, hopefully, established the distinctions between soul and spirit, it would not be unseemly to ask: -"Why does the soul and spirit need to be divided?" This question will be addressed in later chapters, but in the meanwhile we engage in a discussion of the spiritual aspect of the soul which, remember, renders us self-conscious. How are we self-aware? We have intellect, we are aware of self-will; we are aware that we have memory; we are aware that we can make judgements, and we are aware that we have emotions. That these are functions of the human spirit as can be ascertained from the scriptures: -" For who knows a person's thoughts except their own spirit within them? In the same way no one knows the thoughts of God except the Spirit of God."[19] "Watch and pray so that you will not fall into temptation. The spirit is willing, but the flesh is weak."[20]

So there you have it; intellect, will, memory, reason, judgement, and emotion; all functions of the human spirit as testified to in scripture. As has been discussed already, the fruit of the Holy Spirit is love (agapé); joy, peace, patience, kindness, goodness, faithfulness, gentleness and self-control. Let us contrast this with some quotes which will begin to open the door as to why soul and spirit need to be separated: - "Those who are wayward in spirit will gain understanding; those who complain will accept instruction."[21] "I remembered you, God, and I groaned; I meditated, and my spirit grew faint."[22] "David was greatly distressed because the men were talking of stoning him; each one was bitter in spirit because of his sons and daughters."[23] "I will go and be a deceiving spirit in the mouths of all his prophets."[24] "Woe to the foolish prophets who follow their own spirit and have seen nothing!"[25] These do not reflect those who manifest fruit of the Holy Spirit. There are many, many other examples in scripture but the vagaries of translation may deflect some from understanding that the spirit of man, as defined above, is frequently read as 'soul' or 'life' or lives. These come from interpretations of the Greek 'psuche' (from which we derive psyche) and the Hebrew 'nephesh". Natural, sensual, worldly, unspiritual, worldly-minded, without the spirit, and 'follow their natural instinct' are other terms used throughout to render the same original words. These are what we define as soulish which is derived from the Greek 'psuchikos' which is the adjective related to psuche. Psyche is the composite of the volitional, mental, and emotional aspects of the spirit of man.

Since we are aware that the soul is tripartite and under two distinct influences, the flesh, and the spirit, we might, now, becoming aware of the need for separation. The influence of the sensual flesh has to be curtailed and the influence of the God-breathed spirit encouraged. Although the dark night of the purgation of the senses has been discussed, it would be more appropriate, now, to amend the nomenclature a bit and suggest that it would be more accurate to describe it as preparation, correction, and restraint. We are unable to totally expurgate the sensual aspect of the soul, we still have all of our senses and even if we were to indulge in extremes of what would be called self-abuse, otherwise justified as 'penance', we cannot overcome every part of our sensual being. This will never be achieved until we are freed from these wretched bodies. Hence, no matter how effective we have been in pursuit of the way in the first part of the dark night, we will still bear imperfections due to memories, habits, false prophesy, false teaching, pride, and vanity disguised as spirituality, and reveal lack of genuine holy fear of the Living God. In the later stages of the path through the dark night the two aspects of the soul will have to be purged together since they are, by definition, inseparable. This, as the original author has pointed out, is a major deterrent to many. Just as the conditions for discipleship, as defined by Jeshua, caused many to leave Him. As Paul stated "I thought like a child, I reasoned like a child. When I became a man, I put away the ways of childhood."[26] The way to maturity is in changing the mindset, of learning how to acquire the mind of Christ, and being totally led by the Spirit. This is a daunting prospect for those still harbouring any of the aforementioned imperfections whether acknowledged or not. "You were taught, with regard to your former way of life, to put off your old self, which is being corrupted by its deceitful desires; to be made new in the attitude of your minds; and to put on the new self, created to be like God in true righteousness and holiness."[27]

The unregenerate, and even the regenerate infants who, for some reason or other are not weaned and still satisfied with milk; not having any taste for having the mind of Christ and being totally led by the Spirit, will find the prospect of the dark night an anathema. The thought of having their whole soul, lock, stock and barrel; emotions, intellect and will totally subject to the Holy Spirit petrifies them. Jeshua stated:- "Why do you call me, 'Lord, Lord,' and do not do what I say?"[28] and "Not everyone who says to me, 'Lord, Lord,' will enter the kingdom of heaven, but only the one who does the will of my Father who is in heaven."[29] Paul told the Corinthians:- "If what has been built survives, the builder will receive a reward. If it is burned up, the builder will suffer loss but yet will be saved, even though only as one escaping through the flames."[30] Anything of the flesh or is soulish are filthy rags and fit only fit for the eternal fire.

Remember that:- "Each of us will give an account of ourselves to God."[31] So it is incumbent upon the believer, especially one who aspires to discipleship, and even more upon one who desires that he or she is doing the will of our Father to be greeted with the words:- "Well done, good and faithful servant! For those who have persevered this far, be encouraged by the fact that you will only have done so through the auspices of the Holy Spirit. You will have done so because although you are in totally unfamiliar territory and experiencing varying degrees of hesitation and uncertainty, He, the Holy Spirit, is guiding you into, and through, the realms of the spirit. You are learning through experience, what you are experiencing is becoming part of your testimony (remember your *testimony* is only valid if it relates to your experience otherwise it is hearsay and not admissible!). If there is no-one who understands what these contemplatives are experiencing, then there is a danger that they might abandon the path or lose faith and courage; they might also be tempted to impede their progress by excessive recourse to their old ways of meditative discourse. Remember the difference between the meditative and the contemplative as defined earlier. This section is designed to encourage those who might be on the verge of floundering, who are beginning to yield to the seductions of satan and self and start to believe that their difficulties are due to negligence or sin, that they are failing God and are subject to His wrath. We reiterate that at this time God is releasing the soul from the bonds of sensuality and carrying it up to the realm of the spirit. If they are tempted to strive for the Spirit, they will lose that Spirit which has been, hopefully, the source of that agapé, joy and shalom of which they have tasted. The way forward is to embrace that passive, contemplative state and to embrace the way of the cross which is death to all things of the flesh; "Then Jesus said to his disciples "Whoever wants to be my disciple must deny themselves and take up their cross and follow me. For whoever wants to save their life will lose it, but whoever loses their life for me will find it."[32] "Therefore, I urge you, brothers and sisters, in view of God's mercy, to offer your bodies as a living sacrifice, holy and pleasing to God; this is your true and proper worship. Do not conform to the pattern of this world but be transformed by the renewing of your mind. Then you will be able to test and approve what God's will is, his good, pleasing, and perfect will."[33] Even Jeremiah foresaw the way of the cross:- "You deceived me, Lord, and I was deceived; you overpowered me and prevailed. I am ridiculed all day long; everyone mocks me. Whenever I speak, I cry out proclaiming violence and destruction. So the word of the Lord has brought me insult and reproach all day long."[34] To abandon the delights of the contemplative spirit is like one who has found the perfect resort only to leave it in order to re-enter it or one who has found the jewel of great price only to discard it in anticipation of finding it again! It is folly!

Those who are subject to the various temptations should feel comforted and put their trust in their living God, you and I are not the first to have walked this path:- "We also glory in our sufferings, because we know that suffering produces perseverance; perseverance, character; and character, hope."[35] Trials and suffering are all part of God's purging of those who seek to have the mind of Christ and to do the Father's will *and only His will.* (Cf: John 15:19/20). God loves a broken and contrite heart, the way to brokenness and contriteness is through the way of the cross, there are no shortcuts, you will not be the first to have trodden this path, the emphasis here is on perseverance! Way back in Deuteronomy God gave you this promise:- "Be strong and courageous. Do not be afraid or terrified because of them, for the Lord your God goes with you, he will never leave you nor forsake you."[36] Confirmation, along with more sound advice regarding carnality in Hebrews 13:5:- "Keep your lives free from the love of money and be content with what you have, because God has said, "Never will I leave you; never will I forsake you." Remember though, that nearly all of God's promises are conditional, you need to satisfy the conditions before you can claim the promises; if you are this far however, it is likely that, in you, the conditions will largely have been met. It is likely that, although you are not sensing or feeling it, God is saying "well done my true and faithful servant but we have a way to go yet, and I have to do what needs to be done in order to make you fit for moving further into the dark night of the spirit which is the subject of following chapters". This fitness requires freedom of the soul, freedom from the impediment of corporeal activities and freedom from the need to do 'stuff' for God. It takes a major step to abandon this need as, has been said, the flesh and the enemy will try to heap condemnation upon you but "there is now no condemnation for those who are in Christ Jesus."[37] To think that God 'needs' you to do anything is pure arrogance, did He not create the whole heavens and earth without any help from you? Do you think that the fulfilment of His perfect plan relies on you? If so I refer you, once again to Ephesians "In him we were also chosen, having been predestined according to the plan of him who works out everything in conformity with the purpose of his will."[38] It is His desire only that you do His will as testified to by Jeshua earlier, as He has told us:- "Does the Lord delight in burnt offerings and sacrifices as much as in obeying the Lord? To obey is better than sacrifice, and to heed is better than the fat of rams."[39] Only in the divinely sensitised state of the spirit can one distinctly hear the Word of God by which one is brought to a state of faith and without faith one is unable to please God. "Consequently, *faith comes from hearing the message,* and the message is heard through the word about Christ." Notice that the word here is rhematos which implies 'God breathed'; "Without faith it is impossible to please God, because anyone who comes to him must believe that he exists and that He rewards those who earnestly seek him."[40] Those who are still under the influences of carnality will be unable to hear God clearly, and consequently will not understand what His will is, and so will not be able to please Him. That is why He is intent on taking those who are fitted through into the dark night of the spirit.

If one is tempted to become agitated by inactivity and quiet it is prudent to consider the consequences of activity and disquiet; they would detract from those virtues of agapé, joy and shalom evident in the condition of the contrite heart. Consider the case of one posing as a model for a sculptor, the piece is underway and the artist starting to work on some of the more demanding and detailed aspects of the figure being sculpted; then the model gets uncomfortable and starts to shift and move about, maybe even gets up and goes for a wander around. This activity would certainly impede the progress of the project, it would disrupt, prejudice the integrity, and possibly bring about the abandonment of the whole enterprise. Accordingly, it should not fall to the penitent to accede to these temptations and prejudice the work of the Holy Spirit, which is to build up the body of Christ, individually and corporately, and to glorify the Father insofar as the body of believers, obedient, broken, and contrite, and as clay in the potter's hands is caused to grow.

That fire and passion which is agapé love is not always experienced at the start, either because it has not been able to take hold, as in a well laid hearth, or because the hearth is not well prepared, or because the fuel is still damp from the effects of the environment from which it has been garnered. However, in spite of these faults the soul will become more and more sensitive to the delights and attraction of agapé without having any real understanding of the origin of such an exquisite conceptualisation, but as the fire takes hold, the passion and longing will become more intense and zealous. Such a testimony is recorded by King David:- "When my heart was grieved and my spirit embittered, I was senseless and ignorant; I was a brute beast before you. Yet I am always with you; you hold me by my right hand. You guide me with your counsel, and afterward you will take me into glory."[41] This is part of his testimony of having gone through the dark night. Further enlightenment is to be found earlier; "All day long I have been afflicted, and every morning brings new punishments. If I had spoken out like that, I would have betrayed your children. When I tried to understand all this, it troubled me deeply till I entered the sanctuary of God; then I understood their final destiny. Surely you place them on slippery ground; you cast them down to ruin. How suddenly are they destroyed, completely swept away by terrors! They are like a dream when one awakes; when you arise, Lord, you will despise them as fantasies."[42] David has earlier bemoaned the apparent opulence of the immoral, corrupt, and unGodly; he says in verse 13:- "Surely in vain I have kept my heart pure and have washed my hands in innocence." He is sharing his awareness that his dark night experience (entering the sanctuary) empowers him to experience God's wisdom and understanding. He becomes aware of what God has in store for those who are addicted to carnality; David experiences a deep thirst for the living water:- "My soul thirsts for God, for the living God. When can I go and meet with God?"[43] The wise man points out that having such a raging thirst for living water is a great asset, but thirst can also kill, dehydration can be fatal and it the dehydration of the senses that will put to death all addiction to them. It is in the midst of the trial of the dark night of the senses that this wonderful and liberating truth is revealed by the Holy Spirit:- "My sacrifice, O God, is a broken spirit; a broken and contrite heart you, God, will not despise."[44] Again! as testified to by King David. This is the *only* sacrifice acceptable to God, the sacrifice offered in a spirit of solicitude, heartbreak, and humility!

One of the many benefits accrued from the experience is grace; David, once he understood the destiny of the Godless was endued with grace, he did not judge them but left their destiny in the hands of God whilst he got on with his life. Surely *you* place them on slippery ground, *you* cast them down to ruin. David, as do those who traverse the dark night, is acutely aware that *it is by grace alone* that he has been enabled to persevere and endure the trials, and, that having done so, he is empowered to dispense that grace to whomsoever is in need of it. Those to whom this grace has been conceded are not many, the way is hard and most demanding, the trials and tribulations appear never-ending which, of course, they are. The cost, as discussed earlier, is everything, that is why Jeshua warned us: -" But small is the gate and narrow the road that leads to life, and only a few find it."[45] The narrow gate is the dark night of the senses in which the soul is stripped of its addiction to sensual activities so that, empowered by faith alone, it may continue along the narrow way which is the dark night of the spirit.

The benefits of the purgation of the senses may be, to begin with, fairly obscure, but in the heavenlies there is rejoicing, as there is in the case of the new birth, in the weaning of the infant and the abandonment of the need for comforters and nappies (diapers). "The child *grew and was weaned*, and on the day that Isaac was weaned Abraham held a great feast."[46] The time is come to stop sucking at the breast, put aside the milk and ingest solid food; to cause the babe to stop relying on the strong arms of the Father to support him or her and to encourage the infant to walk on its own two feet. We can observe this principle in action when Jeshua sent out the seventy-two: - "Do not take a purse or bag or sandals; and do not greet anyone on the road."[47] This is the way of those being taken through the dark night, abandon the sensual, money, food or clothing and do not seek the counsel of anyone, you must be totally reliant on *me*, says our saviour. The disciple *must* acknowledge his or her total reliability on Christ, they must learn to become totally dependent on *Him*, they must be weaned from the corporeal and worldly. He did not say it would be easy, in fact he forewarned them of the dangers, trials and tribulations they might experience, He had just warned them: "Go, I am sending you out like lambs among wolves." Even in the days of the sojourn in the wilderness the Israelites experienced the purging of the baubles of the flesh: - "Tell the Israelites, 'You are a stiff-necked people. If I were to go with you even for a moment, I might destroy you. Now take off your ornaments and I will decide what to do with you. So, the Israelites stripped off their ornaments at Mount Horeb."[48] If those who presume to have 'leadership' today were to emulate Moses in his pastoral role, the Body of Christ would shine a lot brighter. Sadly our 'leadership', for the most part, are saddled with the sheer encumbrances of their own 'bling' and are thus, unlike Moses, not in any position to pass on the whole Word of God.

The penitent will have to face his own Mount Horeb before he can continue along the narrow way. Abandoning the trinkets and ornaments will assist the soul in appreciating its own miserable state outside the grace of God, how low it had fallen, and how the illumination it had enjoyed in its spiritual indulgences, for that is what they were, was only as having seen through a glass darkly. "For now we see only a reflection as in a mirror; then we shall see face to face. Now I know in part; then I shall know fully, even as I am fully known."[49] 1 Corinthians was one of Paul's earlier letters, it is likely, on reading his later works that he got to know more fully as he traversed his own dark night, for he speaks of the much deeper things of the spirit such as praying in the spirit beyond the boundaries of our language and understanding. The writer to the Hebrews much later emphasised the need for the weaning process: - "In fact, though by this time you ought to be teachers, you need someone to teach you the elementary truths of God's word all over again. *You need milk, not solid food!*"[50]

From now on the penitent will have a far more valid testimony because he will actually be able to testify on the basis of his self-knowledge. He will have a much healthier respect and genuine fear of God, which is as it should be since God is quite capable of vengeance and retribution towards those who cause Him offence without penitence and attrition. For those who doubt, it is to be recommended that you make a study of the whole of scripture in order to derive some understanding of the whole nature of God. For babies to display disrespect and presumption might be forgivable in the eyes of the Father but there is no doubt that He does not tolerate such affront from the more mature as demonstrated in the case of Ananias and Saphira:- "Then Peter said, "Ananias, how is it that satan has so filled your heart that you have lied to the Holy Spirit and have kept for yourself some of the money you received for the land?. Didn't it belong to you before it was sold? And after it was sold, wasn't the money at your disposal? What made you think of doing such a thing? You have not lied just to human beings but to God. When Ananias heard this, he fell down and died. And great fear seized all who heard what had happened."[51] The same fate befell Saphira, his wife, later for the same sin to which she had been party. Some criteria for how someone should approach almighty God is to be discerned from the record of Moses' encounter as recorded in Exodus: "Do not come any closer," God said. "Take off your sandals, for the place where you are standing is holy ground. Then He said, "I am the God of your father, the God of Abraham, the God of Isaac and the God of Jacob." At this, Moses hid his face, because he was afraid to look at God."[52] Those who approach God without all due reverence and respect will not be able to follow the narrow way.

Images of God as a geriatric benefactor must be abandoned because any image which is generated by the human mind is, by its fleshy nature, blasphemous. Since God is purely and exclusively spirit, except in the case of Jeshua, He can only be discerned in the spirit as an entity or individual, He cannot be 'seen' in the common sense, only what is often described, though not in scripture, as 'shekinah' can be 'seen' in any sense. This was the case with the Israelites who saw God as a pillar, of cloud by day, and of fire by night; the effect was startling!:- "Whenever the people saw the pillar of cloud standing at the entrance to the tent, they all stood and worshipped, each at the entrance to their tent."[53] The Lord would speak to Moses face to face, as one speaks to a friend.[54] But at best Moses could have only experienced the shekinah as "He said, "you cannot see my face, for *no one may see me and live.*"[55] This is a definitive statement so any experience involving a 'face to face' encounter with God such as experienced by Moses and again by Isaiah "In the year that King Uzziah died, I saw the Lord, high and exalted, seated on a throne; and the train of his robe filled the temple."[56] This testimony cannot involve an actual sighting of God, only of His glory. The train of His robe, that is the skirts of His robe, filled the whole temple, what Isaiah could see was a manifestation of the glory of God which shook the temple, filled it with smoke and rendered the prophet stricken with conviction." Holy, holy, holy is the Lord Almighty; the whole earth is full of his glory. At the sound of their voices the doorposts and thresholds shook, and the temple was filled with smoke. "Woe to me!" I cried. "I am ruined! For I am a man of unclean lips, and I live among a people of unclean lips, and my eyes have seen the King, the Lord Almighty."[57] Hardly a testimony of one having 'seen' a geriatric benefactor in a white frock! "Therefore, my dear friends, as you have always obeyed, not only in my presence, but now much more in my absence, continue to work out your salvation with fear and trembling."[58] Also translated as deep reverence and awe. It is incumbent upon the believer to have a healthy and respectful, genuine fear of God as He is the ultimate judge and sole juror who holds every part of one's life in His hand. And, as confirmed by so many testimonies in the scriptures, can, and is quite likely to, exercise retribution and vengeance upon those who displease Him. Among those will be the ones identified by Jeshua in Matthew 7:21:- "Not everyone who says to me, 'Lord, Lord,' will enter the kingdom of heaven, but only the one who does the will of my Father who is in heaven."

Note how many of God's promises are conditional as is the one prophesied by Isaiah with regard to the successful negotiation of the dark night:- "If you spend yourselves in behalf of the hungry and satisfy the needs of the oppressed, then your light will rise in the darkness, and your night will become like the noonday[59] God will reveal many truths to the successful pilgrim, not only concerning His majesty, splendour and grandeur as discussed in the last chapter, but also of the pilgrim's own desperate condition apart from the grace of God. Such an awareness is desirable to enable the edict of Nehemiah to be brought to the appropriate conclusion:- "Go and enjoy choice food and sweet drinks and send some to those who have nothing prepared. This day is holy to our Lord. Do not grieve, for the joy of the Lord is your strength."[60] Only when we have the full realisation of His awesome majesty and our own unconscionable state outside of Christ can we enter that state of exquisite joy which is our strength. It is this 'joy unspeakable' which is part of the fruit of the spirit which is discussed earlier. It sustains us throughout the journey and is brought to ultimate fruition in this life when our light is so strong that it violates the darkness and enables the disciple to fulfil his or her commission to spend on behalf of the hungry and satisfy the needs of the oppressed. "See, I lay a stone in Zion, a tested stone, a precious cornerstone for a sure foundation; the one who relies on it will never be stricken with panic. I will make justice the measuring line and righteousness the plumb line; hail will sweep away your refuge, the lie, and water will overflow your hiding place. Your covenant with death will be annulled; your agreement with the realm of the dead will not stand. When the overwhelming scourge sweeps by, you will be beaten down by it. As often as it comes it will carry you away; morning after morning, by day and by night, it will sweep through."[61] Isaiah has warned of the cost of following Christ in the role of disciple, he has foreseen the way of the dark night and endeavoured to prepare the soul in a small way for the rigours and demands of the experience. "And these also stagger from wine and reel from beer: Priests and prophets stagger from beer and are befuddled with wine; they reel from beer, they stagger when seeing visions, they stumble when rendering decisions. All the tables are covered with vomit and there is not a spot without filth. "Who is it he is trying to teach? To whom is he explaining his message? To children weaned from their milk, to those just taken from the breast?"[62] Here the awe-full truth is revealed that attachment to sensory pleasures is as filthy rags in the sight of God and for those being weaned it is necessary to abandon them as was acknowledged by King David:- "You, God, are my God, earnestly I seek you; I thirst for you, my whole being longs for you, in a dry and parched land where there is no water. I have seen you in the sanctuary and beheld your power and your glory."[63] David's testimony is that the knowledge of the shekinah of God came not from the many spiritual delights he had experienced but from the time spent in the parched and desert land; the way to the revelation of the shekinah was not by means of the understanding *but by the way of aridity and barrenness.*

Out of this same aridity and barrenness also comes humbleness which is the product of self-knowledge and the revelation of our state of grace discussed above which precludes vanity, judgmentalism and self-righteousness. Out of this state of humbleness comes a love for the neighbour which they had not been able to articulate hitherto because of the corporeality of their spiritual endeavours. "I will watch my ways and keep my tongue from sin; I will put a muzzle on my mouth while in the presence of the wicked. So, I remained utterly silent, not even saying anything good. But my anguish increased; my heart grew hot within me. While I meditated, the fire burned; then I spoke with my tongue."[64] So says David following his wilderness experience. He became silent, humbled by what had been revealed to him, and his anguish increased perhaps because of his realisation of how far he had had to go in order to acquire the knowledge that he had been given. The vice of spiritual pride is put to death.

David epitomises the dark night in Psalm 77, one makes no apology for quoting this prophet at length as it is the Word of the Lord and "All Scripture is God-breathed and is useful for *teaching, rebuking, correcting and training in righteousness,*"[65] "The word of God is alive and active. Sharper than any double-edged sword, it penetrates even to dividing soul and spirit, joints and marrow; it judges the thoughts and attitudes of the heart."[66] Jeshua sanctioned such sentiments as recorded by Luke:- "Blessed rather are those who hear the word of God and obey it."[67] So it is incumbent upon the pilgrim to note well David's testimony; "When I was in distress, I sought the Lord; at night I stretched out untiring hands, and I would not be comforted. I remembered you, God, and I groaned; I meditated, and my spirit grew faint. You kept my eyes from closing; I was too troubled to speak. I thought about the former days, the years of long ago; I remembered my songs in the night. My heart meditated and my spirit asked: "Will the Lord reject forever? Will he never show his favour again? Has his unfailing love vanished forever? Has his promise failed for all time? Has God forgotten to be merciful? Has he in anger withheld his compassion?" Then I thought, "To this I will appeal: the years when the Most High stretched out his right hand. I will remember the deeds of the Lord; yes, I will remember your miracles of long ago. I will consider all your works and meditate on all your mighty deeds." Your ways, God, are holy. What god is as great as our God?[68] The way, as defined by David, is exclusive and obligatory for the dedicated disciple. All this in the cause of offering the perfect sacrifice:- The sacrifice of a broken spirit; a broken and contrite heart which, God, will not despise."

Such is the way of the purgation of the senses, it may be the case, as in that of Paul, that even one who has known the dark night has to be constantly reminded of the height of his calling and not to be seduced into his former ways; "Therefore, in order to keep me from becoming conceited, I was given a thorn in my flesh, a messenger of satan, to torment me."[69] It is apparent from Paul's other testimonies that he considered this affliction to stand him in good stead:- "But He said to me, "My grace is sufficient for you, for my power is made perfect in weakness." Therefore, I will boast all the more gladly about my weaknesses, so that Christ's power may rest on me."[70] He also advocated the dark night experience for the purging of his contemporaries:- "Hand this man (the sinner consumed by his lust) over to satan for the destruction of the flesh, so that his spirit may be saved on the day of the Lord."[71] Such sentiment is reflected in Isaiah:- "Where are your wise men now? Let them show you and make known what the Lord Almighty has planned against Egypt. The officials of Zoan have become fools, the leaders of Memphis are deceived; the cornerstones of her peoples have led Egypt astray. The Lord has poured into them a spirit of dizziness; they make Egypt stagger in all that she does, as a drunkard staggers around in his vomit."[72] The closing of this chapter might well befall to another of the prophets, Jeremiah: "You disciplined me like an unruly calf, and I have been disciplined. Restore me, and I will return, because you are the Lord my God."[73] AMEN!!!

CHAPTER 20

JOINTS FROM MARROW-A TWO-EDGED SWORD

"For the word of God is alive and active. Sharper than any double-edged sword, it penetrates even to dividing soul and spirit, joints, and marrow; it judges the thoughts and attitudes of the heart." It is deemed advisable to repeat the quote from the letter to the Hebrews as this the focus of the whole of this chapter. We shall discuss the whole sentence a phrase at a time beginning with 'joints and marrow'. This is a most apt metaphor for the preceding phrase 'soul and spirit'. Consider the skeleton and the relationship between joints and marrow; the joints are components of that part which actually provides physical support for the whole body, the marrow is the inner component of some bones which, among other functions, generates blood cells. Red blood cells carry vital life-sustaining oxygen around the body and the white ones safeguard it from infection. Getting access to the marrow, if harvested from the bone, is a painful process, even with modern surgical methods and devices. It is usually carried out under general anaesthetic. Even with the resources of many exegetes and analysts it is difficult to be conclusive with regard to what the Holy Spirit is saying with regard to this metaphor. But what is being said, regardless of historical context is that separating joint from marrow is extremely painful, if it is to be carried out surgically the scalpel has to be sharper than a two-edged sword.

"Blessed are the poor in spirit, for theirs is the kingdom of heaven."[1] Stated our Saviour right at the beginning of what are known as 'the beatitudes'. He had already called those who were to be His disciples to leave their nets, abandon their material possessions, and follow Him. Now He was teaching the about another poverty which would be required of them, poverty of spirit. The way of those who 'hunger and thirst' after righteousness is by way of the dark night which is the second part of this discourse and involves that part of the soul which is the self-centred spirit. They must become 'poor in spirit', they must root from their souls all sense of possessing. Then they will have reached an inner condition comparable to the outer state of the beggars and outcasts who likely made up a significant proportion of those multitudes who had come to hear His words. This is to be taken essentially seriously, for it is the poor in spirit; *theirs* is the kingdom of heaven. Those who would emulate the sentiments of the prophet "The Sovereign Lord is my strength; he makes my feet like the feet of a deer; he enables me to tread on the heights."[2] and those seeking to be able to echo the sentiments of the preceding 18 verses of chapter 3 of Habakkuk must make their way upward through the dark night on the mountain in order to reach those heights to which he was referring. Only from those heights can a soul perceive and experience the deeper mysteries of the spirit. From here he can see great vistas of revelation with great clarity. Only on those heights does one sense the absolute security of having spiritual 'hinds' feet', the sure footedness which comes from having absolute truth revealed to them. The soul of a man desirous of becoming poor in spirit must be cleansed of all memories, habits, thoughts, tastes, emotions, exercises of will, judgements, aspirations and satisfaction which have not been sanctioned by the Holy Spirit and thus sanctified.

This principle is no more plainly illustrated than in the testimony of Abraham. Isaac, his son, was a miracle; on being informed by God of the impending conception of Isaac, "Abraham fell facedown; he laughed and said to himself, "Will a son be born to a man a hundred years old? Will Sarah bear a child at the age of ninety?"[3] The baby, Isaac, embodied everything that was soulish about Abraham; his aspirations in the promises of God, his memories, probably especially those where he had tried to bring those promises to fruition by virtue of his own strength. His intellect and understanding, habits, tastes, emotions, will and judgement and satisfaction; all needed to be dealt with in the cause of having soul and spirit severed by the two-edged sword which is the Word of God. The Word of God took Abraham to the darkest of dark places:- "Then God said, "Take your son, your only son, whom you love, Isaac, and go to the region of Moriah. Sacrifice him there as a burnt offering on a mountain I will show you."[4] Can one imagine the intensity of the anguish which engulfed Abraham as these words penetrated into his soul? He was an old man and had walked a long time in the presence of his God, no doubt he would have much sooner laid down his own life than see, so far as his own understanding would enable him, God's promises brought to nought and all his aspirations invalidated. He was most likely totally bewildered, perhaps, just for a moment, he thought that he may not have heard correctly, but he had walked a long time with his God and knew His voice. It is incumbent upon the believer who is anxious to become poor in spirit to have walked with his Lord long enough to recognise His voice; to have climbed the lower slopes of the mountain and to have endured the trials and purging whilst passing through the less intense time of the dark night.

Abraham knew his Heavenly Father well enough to know what his response had to be. He would make the sacrifice and then trust God to raise Isaac from the dead, this would be the only way whereby God's promises and his aspirations could be fulfilled. "Abraham reasoned that God could even raise the dead, and so in a manner of speaking he did receive Isaac back from death."[5] So reasoned the writer to the Hebrews; the 'manner of speaking' was the reprieve of Isaac: "Do not lay a hand on the boy," He said. "Do not do anything to him. Now I know that you fear God, because you have not withheld from me your son, your only son."[6] Now they both knew the true depth of their relationship, Abraham had demonstrated in the most extraordinary manner his utter devotion and obedience to his God. He had been prepared to abandon absolutely everything. He was a wealthy and influential man, he had sheep, cattle, tents, slaves, servants, an extended family, and was acquainted with kings. Yet in this one act he became poor in spirit, he may have had a lot of 'stuff' but he *possessed* nothing! "I", "me", and "mine" never again meant the same to our belovéd patriarch. The sense of possession was forever purged from his soul. 'Things', which include relationships and talents and gifts, both spiritual and corporeal, have all to be taken up the mountain and put to death on the altar of burnt offerings. The altar of burnt offerings is where 'possessions' are irretrievably destroyed, surrendered to and in the presence of the Living God.

It is in this darkest of dark places that the soul experiences the most intense illumination, the light of revelation penetrates into the deepest parts of the spirit. God secretly teaches the soul and introduces it to the nearest it can get, while still embroiled in the body, to the exquisite delights of agapé and shalom. These delights are infused into the soul without it taking any active part or resorting to any process of natural understanding. Darkness and light become simultaneously present and become supernaturally integrated. David said, "Clouds and thick darkness surround him; righteousness and justice are the foundation of his throne."[7] This is not a statement of fact, as we know that;- "The Lord wraps himself in light as with a garment; he stretches out the heavens like a tent."[8] The earlier Psalm refers to the fact that the light referred to later blinds us because of our pitiful lack of understanding, David further attempted to convey some of his own experience of the dark night:- "He shrouded himself in darkness, veiling his approach with dark rain clouds. Out of the brightness of his presence clouds advanced, with hailstones and bolts of lightning."[9] The thick black clouds of fleshy intellect have to be pierced by the blinding light of revelation.

It is only in the deepest recesses of the soul that light and darkness cohabit, otherwise they cannot! "Do not be yoked together with unbelievers. For what do righteousness and wickedness have in common? Or what fellowship can light have with darkness?"[10] The context is particular, but the principle is universal, sin and righteousness cannot co-exist. Paul later quoted the prophet Isaiah:- "Therefore, "Come out from them and be separate, says the Lord. Touch no unclean thing, and I will receive you."[11,12] Part of the necessity of the purging is to provide the pilgrim with the power to live the victorious life. "Everyone born of God overcomes the world. This is the victory that has overcome the world, even our faith."[13] We know that satan has license from two sources, from God[14-16] and from the individual through sin. "If we deliberately keep on sinning after we have received the knowledge of the truth, no sacrifice for sins is left."[17] Note that one is still deliberately sinning if one does not actively live in a penitent state; if one does note continuously pray the prayer of David:- "Put me on trial, Lord, and cross-examine me. Test my motives and my heart."[18] This would be a matter of course for those who genuinely seek truth, who hunger and thirst after righteousness and who desire to be poor in spirit. Many do not have such holy motivation and consider themselves not to be in need of purging of the soul; this, of course is vanity, pride, and arrogance, some of those vices which are abhorrent to the Living God, and open doors for demonic influences to run amok in a believer. Amok means to attack furiously, a wild frenzy, run about in a wild manner or a murderous frenzy- take your pick!

"All was well with me, but he shattered me; he seized me by the neck and crushed me. He has made me his target."[19] God had licensed satan to test Job, as He Himself had tested Abraham. Job too was a very wealthy man, his livestock was counted in thousands, he feared God, shunned evil and was considered blameless and upright. But, by his own confession, God had 'shattered' and 'crushed' him. Both these men suffered in order that they be made broken and contrite, this is because it is the broken and contrite heart that is so dear to God, it is the pilgrim who has been rendered poor in spirit who is close to the Father's heart. "The sacrifice you desire is a broken spirit. You will not reject a broken and repentant heart, O God."[20] The prophetic pronouncement made by King David, a verse so tragically bypassed by many a pilgrim, not comprehending the absolute necessity of allowing it to suffuse into their spirits. Both of these men experienced the realisation of what Jeshua was to tell humanity centuries later:- "I'll say it again, it is easier for a camel to go through the eye of a needle than for a rich person to enter the Kingdom of God!"[21] Whatever discussions are entered into regarding camels and eyes of needles, what is blatantly apparent is that is that riches are an insurmountable obstacle! What a rich person or territory is primarily described as having, is an abundance of material wealth such as describes our two Godly forebears. The dictionaries will also define richness or wealth as embracing intellectual, emotional and spiritual property, rich traditions, a rich baritone voice, rich in ideas, rich in compassion, etcetera. All these and many other purely ethereal concepts can legitimately be described as riches.

We can now put these testimonies, and those of a multitude of other pilgrims, into the context of the dark night experience, it is not sufficient to just surrender the demands of the senses to our God, it is essential to surrender the demands of the soul too! We have to come to the place where *all of our possessions* are to be put on the altar of burnt offerings! Every promise, every memory, every emotion, every blood tie, every soul tie, every aspiration; every fragment of satisfaction and sense of achievement, every self-congratulatory thought and every hint of smugness and self-justification. Particularly difficult is this challenge for those who think that they have become 'qualified' in some way through their various 'ministries' for exemption from the trials of the dark night. Only those who have already survived those trials are actually 'qualified' to minister in the power of the Holy Spirit because they consider themselves having been raised from the dead in the manner of speaking related by the writer to the Hebrews quoted earlier. They are the ones who can *testify* to their having died and been born anew, and this fact will be evidenced by their fruit-bearing! 'Qualification' does not involve having gone through a rite or ritual nor the bearing of any insignia or establishment of status. Anyone who has the necessary experience and through that experience acquired necessary skills is qualified. Anyone who has the necessary surgical skills can do surgery even if they have never attended medical school or have done so but been struck off! It does not matter! the end result is that they bring and sustain life! This is the fundamental principle of body ministry as stressed throughout scripture and particularly in chapter 4 of the letter to the church at Ephesus.

Those who consider that they have a special 'calling' or are otherwise exclusive are already evidencing the sins of pride and vanity and probably other fruits of thorn bushes and thistles. We are all holy priests: "As you come to him, the living Stone, rejected by humans but chosen by God and precious to him; you also, like living stones, are being built into a spiritual house to be a holy priesthood, offering spiritual sacrifices acceptable to God through Jesus Christ."[22] "This, then, is how you ought to regard us: as servants of Christ and as those entrusted with the mysteries God has revealed."[23] Paul is testifying as one who has known the dark night and to whom has been revealed the deep mysteries of the spirit, *not* one who is distributing milk, he regards himself, as always, as a servant:- "Not lording it over those entrusted to you, but being examples to the flock."[24]

Such souls will be those who may appear to have much but who possess nothing. Note that the 'fortunes' of both men in our citation had their fortunes restored. We are told:- "Do not worry, saying, 'What shall we eat?' or 'What shall we drink?' or 'What shall we wear?' For the pagans run after all these things, and your heavenly Father knows that you need them. But *seek first* his kingdom and his righteousness, and all these things will be given to you *as well*."[25] Those who preach 'prosperity' as a means of attracting the gullible to 'give their lives to Christ' are among the most repugnant to the Living God; theirs is one of the many blasphemies being perpetrated throughout various congregations in the present day. Absolutely contrary to all teaching to be found in scripture, we have learned, hopefully, that only *after* having abandoned all notions of wealth and standing does the pilgrim make *any* spiritual progress. Anyone preaching or subscribing to this heresy has opened the door to all sorts of demonic influences. This is because their 'commitment' is based on carnal desire, that of lust after 'stuff', God will always provide for the needs of His children but never their wants! No-one can make any sort of deal with God, only enter into a covenant with Him in which they offer their whole life in an act of total and unconditional surrender. Only when one has subscribed to this condition can they experience that divine mystery that, having given up everything; they have gained everything but possess nothing. Only those who possess nothing have effectively closed the door to any demonic influences which might have gained access through unrecognised or unacknowledged sin. Only those who possess nothing can stand in the blinding light and be aware of that shaft of darkness through which they were enabled to survive such intense light. Only those who Father acknowledges as being pure in heart; "Blessed are the pure in heart, for they will see God."[26] They can enter through the eye of a needle, but they will have to have abandoned their camels.

Some, when confronted with the onset of the dark night, are liable to think that they have proven to be unworthy of God. They become miserable and distraught, they know not why, but suppose that they have become set against His way, and it causes them a deal of grief and pain. In despair they will rail against God in their confusion and misunderstanding of His ways. "If I have sinned, what have I done to you, you who see everything we do? Why have you made me your target? Have I become a burden to you?"[27] cried out our great mentor, Job. The intense light has penetrated the darkness of his condition and illuminated all of that which is soulish and impure, he considers himself unworthy and a burden. This is a moment of acute agony for the soul thinks itself now totally unworthy of God, fit only for torture and rejection because it now realises that within the constrictions of his soulishness, that is in his own strength, worthiness and restoration are unattainable. "When you rebuke and discipline anyone for their sin, you consume their wealth like a moth, surely everyone is but a breath."[28] To quote King David again, It is possible that one might be so overcome with melancholy in the midst of the dark night that their focus becomes intensified so that their one desire becomes 'let us get it over and done with; call me home Father',

"There the upright can establish their innocence before him, and there I would be delivered forever from my judge."[29]

Suffering is an *essential* feature of the Christian life: - "Now if we are children then we are heirs of God and co-heirs with Christ, if indeed we share in His sufferings in order that we may also share in His glory[30] And father has all sorts of reasons for allowing us suffering. He is "The Father of compassion and the God of all comfort, who comforts us all in our troubles, so that we can comfort those in any trouble with the comfort we ourselves receive from God[31] and "They preached the gospel in that city and won a large number of disciples. Then they returned to Lystra, Iconium and Antioch strengthening the disciples and encouraging them to remain true to the faith. "We must go through many hardships to enter the kingdom of God," they said."[32] Quoting Paul and Barnabas. Suffering is also essential in the cause of acquiring purity of soul and spirit; "We also glory in our sufferings, because we know that suffering produces perseverance; perseverance, character; and character, hope."[33] We know from Job that he was aware that his suffering was in the greater cause, "Have pity on me, my friends, have pity, for the hand of God has struck me;"[34] he cried. This is par for the course for the would-be disciple "To this you were called, because Christ suffered for you, leaving you an example, that you should follow in his steps."[35] Stated Peter unequivocally. It is vital for the pilgrim to recognise that the way of the dark night is not the means of chastisement and rebuke but the way of liberty, enlightenment and power and authority.

CHAPTER 21

THE AUTHOR AND FINISHER

This is the sentiment expressed by King David: "Where can I go from your Spirit? Where can I flee from your presence?"[1] It had been endorsed by Moses in the song which he had recited before the whole assembly of Israel; "The Lord alone led him; no foreign god was with him."[2] Where the pilgrim is required to go is that very lonely and quiet place whereby the soul can come to the full realisation of the need to abandon reason in order to assimilate the whole word of God. What governs the life of the unpurged believer, reason, or God? On the road to Damascus Paul was blinded. This man was an influential rabbi; we know from his correspondence that he was a pharisee and well educated, having been tutored at the school of Gamaliel founded by Hillel, a most respected and honoured Jewish scholar. He had, as evidenced in his writings, a thorough knowledge of all of the Jewish scriptures and traditions attributable to the high standard of his rabbinic training. The servants of God have to be delivered from the soulishness of reason, they cannot live by sight; the moment that Paul saw the blinding light he had to abandon all of his considerable powers of reason. All of his learning and understanding was cast asunder in one instant by virtue of the blinding light. He had reasoned with his understanding, such as it was, that it was not only 'reasonable,' but his responsibility to go about murdering Christians! Anyone who is not delivered from the bondage of reason will become a slanderer, they can always justify their slander on the grounds that they have 'reasoned' their way to some conclusion which, in their opinion, justifies their sin. That is why slander is specifically condemned over 22 times in the Newer Testament alone!

Reason is the first cause of rebellion. But, as rational beings, how can we refrain from reasoning? Especially reasoning with God; this sounds almost absurd, that is why we have to pay particular attention to the purging of our reason. The question answers itself in the proposition that it is unreasonable to expect anyone not to use their powers of reason! But there are two distinct categories of Christian, those who live on the lower plane of reason and those who live on the higher plane of Godly authority and revelation. The fruit of the tree of the knowledge of good and evil impresses us every time we hear from God, to question the command, to consider the issue and decide if there are sufficient reasons for either doing or not doing what is asked. The fruit of that tree governs every facet of the life of the unpurged soul, everything appointed by God has to be filtered and judged by our reason; we think for our creator and decide what He should think.

Anyone bent on following the pilgrim's path must submit to the purging of his reason, he must live by the rhemata of God or live by the process of human reasoning, it is absolutely impossible to live by both! Of course, reason will say "How can I live without my powers of reason, if I survive, I will be, at best, a lunatic!" No; here we have to recognise the schism which exists between the human and the Divine, if you are going to analyse and reason in this manner you have blundered into a quagmire of your own making. Your reasoning has to be subject to the Holy Spirit, and Him only. We are required to have the mind of Christ, if we are to have the unblemished mind of Christ then the self-centred understanding must, in a manner of speaking, be put to death, it must be abandoned, and the soul must accept that God will provide His own understanding by revelation on 'need to know' basis.

Let us investigate the testimony of the prophet Jonah. If you are questioning the validity of his testimony, you are already exposing your sin, the very reason why this cleansing is essential to you. If you need to understand how he could survive in the belly of a fish and so on, you are trapped; the truth is that you do not need to have an understanding, you do not need to question

174

any of the statements made. What you are trying to do is reduce the Absolute Divine One to something within the realms of your own intellect. It will not do! "You hurled me into the depths, into the very heart of the seas, and the currents swirled about me; all your waves and breakers swept over me. The engulfing waters threatened me, the deep surrounded me; seaweed was wrapped around my head." he cried.[3] Not once did he ask for an explanation, he just acknowledged that he was going through the dark night and surrendered to the will of his Father without question. He, as did all the others, experienced the loneliness and desolation which accompanies the pilgrim through this journey, "To the roots of the mountains I sank down; the earth beneath barred me in forever. But you, Lord my God, brought my life up from the pit."[4] He testified immediately after. The contemplative will find, in the midst of this most intense of distresses, that his loneliness and sense of abandonment are accentuated by the awareness that many of those who had been close to him will have been separated from him by various devices.

God's commandments, that is to 'come out from' or, to remind one of the inferences in the original Hebrew, 'to become *separate*' from. One may find that not so many of those with whom he had enjoyed many times of fellowship are still within his embrace. Those who are still within reach will, unless they have travelled the way themselves aforetime, be of no comfort or solace to the one suffering. The 'friends' of Job proved of no service to him in his darkest hour; King David bemoaned "You have taken from me my closest friends and have made me repulsive to them. I am confined and cannot escape."[5]

The need for isolation is explained by Ezekiel in a parable:- "Then set the empty pot on the coals till it becomes hot and its copper glows, so that its impurities may be melted and its deposit burned away"[6] The soul must first be separated from its contents then the fire of purgation must burn until the pot heats almost to melting point in order that the impurities, (other translations:- filth and corruption, rust, scum and dross), be absolutely eliminated. It is only when the human understanding is dealt with that the glimmers of Divine understanding penetrate into the darkness. Job, in the middle of his discourse, beheld a flicker of enlightenment during his response to his 'friend' Bildad; "Where then does wisdom come from? Where does understanding dwell?"[7] answering his own question a few verses later. "And he said to the human race, The fear of the Lord, that is wisdom, and to shun evil is understanding."[8] Wisdom, the prerequisite accomplice of understanding is to be sought at any cost, so states King Solomon,[9] "The beginning of wisdom is this: Get wisdom. Though it cost all you have, get understanding."[10] It appears that the great, wise King considered wisdom and understanding to be synonymous. He had specifically requested these gifts:- "Give me wisdom and knowledge, that I may lead this people, for who is able to govern this great people of yours?"[11]

True wisdom and understanding and knowledge are spiritual gifts.[12] Human wisdom and understanding is entirely different! "If you harbour bitter envy and selfish ambition in your hearts, do not boast about it or deny the truth. Such 'wisdom' does not come down from heaven but is earthly, unspiritual, demonic."[13] Note well! Wisdom, knowledge and understanding which is not under the total control of the Holy Spirit is straight off of the wrong tree from the garden, all of it, thistles and thorns; knowledge of good and evil! Totally abhorrent to the Living God! "His understanding no one can fathom." Isaiah concluded,[14] In order to understand why we have to surrender our understanding in order to be able to understand, we first have to abandon our need to understand why. This is another of those paradoxes which can only be comprehended fully by the poor in spirit. However, in each of the cases referred to, the ordeal was tempered, eventually, by restitution and recovery. Abraham had all of his household restored, as did Job and King David. Jonah, it seems, allowed anger to obscure all that was to be gleaned from his dark night experience. He allowed his own reason and understanding to provoke him to anger and question God's will, having already demonstrated his rebellion by running off to Tarshish instead of going where he was supposed to, to Nineveh.

He had already decided that God was unreasonable, he had thought to make a decision on behalf of his creator; "He prayed to the Lord, "Isn't this what I said, Lord, when I was still at home? That is what I tried to forestall by fleeing to Tarshish. I knew that you are a gracious and compassionate God, slow to anger and abounding in love, a God who relents from sending calamity."[15] He was trying to justify himself to the Living God, he considered the citizens of Nineveh to be unworthy of His mercy and compassion, he had made a serious error of judgement. He had not understood that God does exactly as He wills and does not involve Himself in soulish debate, He cannot for He is truth. "It does not, therefore, depend on human desire or effort, but on God's mercy." "Therefore, God has mercy on whom he wants to have mercy, and he hardens whom he wants to harden."[16] As Paul told the Romans.

To harden one's heart does not mean that the Father causes one to sin, it means that He has given them up to exercise their free-will do so. "Although they claimed to be wise, they became fools, and exchanged the glory of the immortal God for images made to look like a mortal human being and birds and animals and reptiles. Therefore, God gave them over in the sinful desires of their hearts to sexual impurity for the degrading of their bodies with one another."[17] This condemnation includes those who have made idols of their own intellect and understanding! "One of you will say to me: "Then why does God still blame us? For who is able to resist his will?" But who are you, a human being, to talk back to God? Shall what is formed say to the one who formed it, 'Why did you make me like this?"[18] One very wise and anonymous saint has remarked that he more he lives in glory the less he reasons. If any man reasons a lot, we may know that he has never seen glory. The way to know God is through obedience. All who still live in their reasonings have not known Him. The obedient alone truly know God. Herein is how the knowledge of good and evil which comes from Adam is eliminated. Thereafter it is relatively easy for us to obey.

Lamentations: a whole book full of thoughts, every one focused on the blackness, devastation, humiliation, sorrow, loss and sense of abandonment which are all borne out of sin; this is acknowledged in every chapter. However, as always, God embeds a glimmer of hope; "Though he brings grief, he will show compassion, so great is his unfailing love. For he does not willingly bring affliction or grief to anyone."[19] This is not to say that He is *unwilling* that affliction and grief be brought to bear where necessary, but this is *not* His approbative will, it is His permissive will. As we have observed, many of our Older Testament saints suffered affliction and grief in the cause of their spiritual purity and we are required to walk the same path. "Consider it pure joy, my brothers and sisters, whenever you face trials of many kinds, because you know that the testing of your faith produces perseverance."[20] recommended one apostle, as did his fellow; "We also glory in our sufferings, because we know that suffering produces perseverance; perseverance, character; and character, hope."[21] "He reveals the deep things of darkness and brings utter darkness into the light."[22] For further encouragement King David informs:- "Even the darkness will not be dark to you; the night will shine like the day, for darkness is as light to you.."[23] "When my spirit grows faint within me, it is you who watch over my way. In the path where I walk people have hidden a snare for me."[24] It is profitable to give some thought to all hardships, trials, adversities, and frustrations which have beset anyone who seeks poverty of spirit. They certainly will have experienced such events in various manners and the first thought of one thus engaged should be:- 'Lord what are you trying to teach me in this situation?' 'What is the great spiritual truth to be learned in the midst of these circumstances?'

The answer, to those who have an earnest desire for light and truth and life, will be "I am purifying you to make you more like my Son; to make you Christ-like. I am causing you to understand true humbleness, I am purging you of soulishness, I am making you empty of self and replacing all the dross that was within you with my Holy Spirit." Rebelliousness and resistance to the way of the dark night come from natural reasoning which will have had its collaborator and origin in thought. Hence "We demolish arguments and every pretension that sets itself up against the knowledge of

God, and we take captive every thought to make it obedient to Christ."[25] 'Lofty opinion' and 'presumption' are other terms used in references used to describe the barriers to a deep knowledge of our God. Note that Paul is in the demolition and slavery business, he is tearing down strongholds of the mind in verse 4, and he is taking all thoughts captive so that they might be held under strict supervision! Actually, it is a case of recapturing thoughts and leading them out of the demolished strongholds of satanic influences and to be freed to become willing captives of Jeshua. In a sense, no-one is in a position to exercise their free-will in the normally accepted sense because they are either slaves to sin or slaves to Christ; as has been emphasised earlier, there is no neutral ground, no 'no man's land', "Whoever is not with me is against me, and whoever does not gather with me scatters."[26] stated Jeshua, The one who has had his thoughts and understanding surrendered to Christ will no longer express his opinions but only speak the truth in love. His statements will be authenticated by a thorough knowledge of the *whole* of scripture after the practice and custom of the Bereans.

The Presence of God and the manifestation of the presence of God are not the same, "Where can I go from your Spirit? Where can I flee from your presence? enquired David, answering his own question in the next three verses; "If I go up to the heavens, you are there; if I make my bed in the depths, you are there. If I rise on the wings of the dawn, if I settle on the far side of the sea, even there your hand will guide me, your right hand will hold me fast."[27] He had moved on from witnessing manifestations of His presence through miraculous events and his own, and the testimonies of others, to an absolute consciousness of His omnipresence. Reason, deduction, and understanding had been superseded by faith, even in his darkest hour he was certain of His presence even when there was no manifestation of it. In fact, the certainty of His presence when there are no feelings, signs or wonders involved is what is recognised as faith. Even in the days of calamity said Habakkuk "Yet I will rejoice in the Lord, I will be joyful in God my Saviour. The Sovereign Lord is my strength; he makes my feet like the feet of a deer, he enables me to tread on the heights."[28] Such pilgrims never need sense, thought, emotion or understanding to enjoy, full-time, the manifestation of His presence. An earthly father might say, as his son enters into maturity, 'I feel that my son is starting to draw closer to me now'; even if the boy has grown up supported and nourished by his father; or should I say 'especially? The bonds of love between them will grow and become stronger and they will become closer in mind, heart, and spirit. Of course, this does happen in 'real life', but, since the fall, is more likely to happen in the life of the believer who hungers and thirsts after righteousness. It is the infant who has to grow into the fullest relationship in the Father, the natural child could have to have an innate desire for his relationship with his father to grow to maturity. But he could not think or reason or understand his way into it, as with our way to deep relationship with our heavenly Father; the hunger and thirst and desire has to be there to the extent that we will have to do something about it. It will not come about by our own efforts but because of that aching gap in our spirits, that void left where God had been before the fall causes the believer to cry out "Hear my voice when I call, Lord; be merciful to me and answer me. My heart has heard you say, "Come and talk with me." And my heart responds, "Lord, I am coming. Do not hide your face from me, do not turn your servant away in anger; you have been my helper. Do not reject me or forsake me, God my Saviour."[29]

"Oh, the depth of the riches of the wisdom and knowledge of God! How unsearchable his judgements, and his paths beyond tracing out!"[30] It is necessary to accept such statements as essential truth! Prying into the deep mysteries and paradoxes with which our gracious but enigmatic God surrounds Himself may make theologians, but it will never make a disciple. For those who have had their 'need to know', who have had their reliance on intellect and thought and deduction exterminated, they will be able to taste and see that there are treasures to be gained; good, solid, nourishing life-sustaining meat to be feasted on in the banqueting halls of the Kingdom. Those who have endured the dark night will be royally rewarded. David expressed his wonder on meditating on the enigmatic God "When I consider your heavens, the work of your fingers, the moon and the stars, which you have set in place, what is mankind that you are mindful of them, human beings that you care for them?"[31] Incidentally, here again is evidence of his humbleness, his total acceptance of the need for absolute submission to the will of God. His need for recognition, his vanity, his pride and all have been left on the altar of burnt offerings and been consumed by the fire. Job, on the other hand has, at chapter 12, still had not quite got the message, he acknowledges the wonderful truth which has been revealed to him in the dark night, "He reveals the deep things of darkness and brings utter darkness into the light."[32] But has not allowed that pearl of wisdom to impress itself into his soul and spirit. Five verses later he is exhibiting the classic problem wrought about by the tenacity with which the carnal part of the soul will continue to try and dominate the spirit in man:- "But I desire to speak to the Almighty and to argue my case with God."[33] This reflects the paradigm of many a believer and, has been stated earlier, is an unsurmountable obstacle to many a would-be disciple. As an offer of further encouragement, I would quote a few other saints as testimony that it might be represented by demonic powers as 'unsurmountable' but they are all liars! Eventually Job made it through:- "My ears had heard of you but now my eyes have seen you. Therefore, I despise myself and repent in dust and ashes."[34] That must be one of the most beautiful statements in the Bible. Job had not literally 'seen God', no-one has seen God and lived, this is stated categorically in the scriptures, but the word is used metaphorically several times to emphasise an epiphanic event.

Further testimonies are to be found in the book of Daniel:- "He reveals deep and hidden things; he knows what lies in darkness, and light dwells with him."[35] and "Oh, how great are God's riches and wisdom and knowledge! How impossible it is for us to understand his decisions and his ways!"[36] Jeshua,, in an address to His disciples, told them, "The knowledge of the secrets of the kingdom of God has been given to you, but to others I speak in parables, so that, "though seeing, they may not see; though hearing, they may not understand."[37] This truth was addressed to His *disciples*, recall the only biblical definition of discipleship!

181

"Surely you have heard about the administration of God's grace that was given to me for you, that is, the mystery made known to me by revelation, as I have already written briefly. In reading this, then, you will be able to understand my insight into the mystery of Christ, which was not made known to people in other generations as it has now been revealed by the Spirit to God's holy apostles and prophets."[38] This is in itself a revelation, God's mysteries are revealed through the revelations given to the like of apostles and prophets; all of whom qualified as disciples, all of whom had been through the dark night, and all of whom had been given feet as hind's feet on high places. God has administered to His people through the likes of such men and women throughout the ages.

However, as it is written: "What no eye has seen, what no ear has heard, and what no human mind has conceived, the things God has prepared for those who love him; these are the things God has revealed to us by his Spirit. The Spirit searches all things, even the deep things of God."[39] The Bible is the written word of God and bound by the constraints of paper and ink and the predilections of various translators. Rhemata, on the other hand, are the living Word and under no constraints whatsoever. "The Spirit gives life; the flesh counts for nothing. The words I have spoken to you, they are full of the Spirit and life."[40] The words in the Bible have power only when they have the Spirit of God breathed into them, otherwise they are merely grammata, letters, as Paul says, that kill. Anyone, including satan, can quote chunks of scripture accurately but, unlike the rhemata of God will go forth and return void. Note that Paul has stated unequivocally that 'no eye has seen, no ear heard what God has revealed by His Spirit'. It is the Spirit which gives life, all else brings death; it is the *voice* of God which has to be *heard* and the climb up the mountain and the passage through the dark night are designed to fine-tune the spirit of the pilgrim to the voice of God. Paul is saying that God did not write a book and send it by messenger across ages and continents by unspiritual, soulish minds. Throughout scripture the emphasis is on what God *says*. Of itself the scripture only says that it is *profitable*, not *essential*, the rhema of God affects the hearts of all men; many who have never heard of a Bible have been moved by the Spirit to a state where they have found salvation through Christ. It depends not on the words but on the receptivity of the hearer of the Word which does not go forth and return void! For any believer who does not clearly hear the Spirit speaking, it is because He speaks in a small still voice, and it is easily drowned out by soulish clutter and interference. After all, if God could not, would not, or just did not, speak to His people- what sort of God would He be?

The speaking voice is a fact and the effect it has on the saints from any age to date is testified to by all of them. Jeshua placed some emphasis on the spoken Word, "Whoever has ears, let them hear." He said[41] He used the same phrase on another occasion. However, it seems that among congregations there is a heretical spirit that initiates a propensity towards noise which makes hearing difficult, if not impossible. Being still and knowing that He is God is currently, by and large, out of favour; megawatts, PowerPoint presentations, magnitude, activities, and campaigns are the vogue. Forgotten, it seems, is the admonition that "They who wait for the Lord shall renew their strength; they shall mount up with wings like eagles; they shall run and not be weary; they shall walk and not faint."[42] It is the poor in spirit, those with a broken and contrite heart, who will be totally content to be still and wait for as long as He deems fit. They will long have abandoned all their desires for the above-mentioned soulish pursuits. It is they who will soar into the heavenly places where the deep things of God, mentioned by Paul above, are to be found. It is they who have submitted to and experienced the deep searching and severing of soul and spirit by the Spirit of God who will have been rendered candidates fitted to search the deep things of God.

It is those who have waited, for as long as it takes, who have actually spent enough time in their closet, often translated 'inner room' and waited; this was the recommendation of Jeshua: - "When you pray, go into your inner room, shut your door, and pray to your Father, who is unseen. And your Father, who sees what is done in secret, will reward you."[43] Frequently the reward will be shafts of intense, bright light of revelation piercing the dark confines of the closet. Beams of understanding and knowledge of truth bringing illumination to the pray-er seen much more clearly due to the ambient darkness. It is within the confines of the closet, the sacred place of freedom from sensual distraction that one might acquire a sense of the chasm between the divine and the carnal, the spirit will view its own experiences from an entirely different viewpoint. This is because it is beginning to see through the eyes of Christ, as Paul says: - "Who has known the mind of the Lord so as to instruct him?" But we have the mind of Christ[44]. Brothers and sisters, I could not address you as people who live by the Spirit but as people who are still worldly, mere infants in Christ."[45] Infants, those who are still worldly, cannot be introduced to the deep things of the Spirit, it is impossible because, as has been discussed, riches do not consist only of material things but the ethereal and intangible too. Says Isaiah "As a pregnant woman about to give birth writhes and cries out in her pain, so were we in your presence, Lord."[46] thus probably adequately describing the agonies associated with the transition from embryonic to mature, the conditions are totally different! But having been through the traumas of a dramatic change of circumstances and environment and survived, a soul might, after some time of growth and cultivation, consider his relationship with his creator. He is likely, but not necessarily, to seek to find some time of growth and cultivation, consider his relationship with his creator. He is likely, but not necessarily, to seek to find some answers through the scriptures. But until he is convinced that God is actually a living, vital being and actually anxious for us to make contact with Him, and that He is ready, willing and able to communicate with us on a personal level; he is a victim of double-mindedness and consequently inarticulate. However, the soul who hears the small, still voice and responds out of agapé will, because dwells in the appropriate environment, be able to enter that state of intimate co-existence with the Godhead which the author described as contemplation. The Word of God is no longer to be found solely through a series of characters in a book, but is available at all times, anywhere, - written on the heart and in the spirit of the believer. "You show that you are a letter from Christ, the result of our ministry, written not with ink but with the Spirit of the living God, not on tablets of stone but on tablets of human hearts."[47] Until the *whole* of scripture is written on the heart of an individual it is still only written on a tablet of stone, a hard and intransigent place, unyielding and demanding a great deal of labour and force before the mason can make any impression upon it.

Once the pilgrim has allowed the whole scripture to written on his heart, he will be familiar, through his own testimony, of some of the less palatable truths, those which they with itching ears will go to great pains to avoid. "One who is more powerful than I will come, the straps of whose sandals I am not worthy to untie. He will baptise you with the Holy Spirit and fire."[48,49] What baptism involves has been discussed, what is to be emphasised here is that it is all-consuming! What has also been emphasised is that the Holy Spirit will only occupy territory that has been surrendered to Him- He is not invasive. He can only take over the areas of our lives which have been purged and made clean, made a holy place as befits a dwelling-place for the Holy Spirit. How is this to be achieved? Through fire!

Way back in Deuteronomy we have been warned of what John was concerned about:- "For the Lord your God is a consuming *fire*, a jealous God."[50] warned Moses, (and he should know!) "The Lord will wash away the filth of the women of Zion; he will cleanse the bloodstains from Jerusalem by a spirit of judgement and a spirit of fire."[51] and so should he! In case of there still being a reader with itching ears, arguing that this was only 'Older Testament' stuff. (The dreadful influence of the carnal soul, insisting on using reasoning and understanding!) A quote from the Newer Testament:- "Therefore, since we are receiving a kingdom that cannot be shaken, let us be thankful, and so worship God acceptably with reverence and awe, for our "God is a consuming *fire*."[52] The fire is a euphemism, in this case, for the purging of the soul through the various trials and tribulations discussed, and it is the lot of every soul who hungers and thirsts after righteousness. The foolish and vain will think that if they have not had to suffer the purging, they are already righteous and poor in spirit. Some who have endured some tribulations and so think that a few afflictions of the body or the emotions have qualified them but have not had these soulish experiences separated from their spirit likewise. This is a clear manifestation of the vain, arrogant and soulish spirit which indwells so many and precisely that which is the pilgrim must acknowledge and repent of, else there is no hope! Consider a log and the fire; the fire, in pursuit of totally absorbing and becoming one with the log, must consume it. This is the passion of agapé, the passion of Christ who, having been through all of the most intense agonies of the dark night Himself, asks us to endure them for His sake. "I want to know Christ, yes, to know the power of his resurrection and the fellowship of sharing in his sufferings, becoming like him in his death." Wrote Paul to the Philippians[53], the word he uses for fellowship is the word 'koinonia', it means 'to have in common with.' (Totally different from 'ecclesia' usually translated, in English, as 'church'). First of all, the heat will cause the log to dry out, aridity is often the first stage in the purgation process. As it dries it will give off unpleasant or even foul odours and fumes, it will blacken and become more distressed in both senses of the word; eventually the fire will have reduced the log to a state whereby it can be consumed by and become an integral and functional component of the fire. It will have been baptised into the fire in, possibly, the most explicit and informative analogy of the term that there is. In this transformation the wood is neither active or passive, but both; another paradox involving the fusion of singularity and multiplicity.

Without faith it is impossible to please God, because anyone who comes to him must believe that he exists and that he rewards those who earnestly seek him." So states the writer to the Hebrews.[54] Faith, the writer told us earlier in the chapter is evidence, conviction, certainty, assurance, or proof, (depending on your predisposition), of things unseen. If our faith depends upon anything soulish it does not please God. All the saints quoted during this discourse, whether at one time or not, having evidenced that which they had relied on in the flesh, had overcome, abandoned their soulishness and arrived at the pinnacle on which the victorious can stand with feet as hind's feet on high places. Can we say that faith is a state of continuous consciousness and fellowship, (koinonia- that is 'shared in common'), with the Living God. This is Christlikeness after the manner of Himself who was constantly attentive to and inseparable from His Father, as He has told us in John's gospel.[55] "Faith comes from hearing, and hearing through the word of Christ."[56] Faith comes to those who will be still and listen. Faith comes from constant koinonia with the Godhead; Paul exhorted us "Pray continually, never stop praying, or Pray without ceasing,"[57] take your pick. "And whatever you do, whether in word or deed, do it all in the name of the Lord Jesus, giving thanks to God the Father through him."[58] These admonitions will already have been incorporated into the lives of those who have travelled the way of the dark night, they will have become the norm in their lives, they will have become as spiritual reflexes requiring no more conscious effort. They will have become hardly conscious of their own existence; they will have become so God-centred that they are totally preoccupied with Him and will not be conscious of having been deprived of anything of value during the dark night. All the frustrations, agonies, failures, and miseries will have found profound relief in Christ, having surrendered everything to Him. Soul will have been severed from spirit.

Hopefully, if you have come this far, the discourse can now move on to the secret places as described by the closet and the dark night and investigate the scriptural bases for coming to terms with what we can now recognise as an authentic 'new creation'. We will be in a state of wonderment, of bewilderment in a sense, we will have been spiritually dissected and made transparent, and been made all the more joyous for the experience. We will have been given a divine revelation as to what agapé is:- "To love the Lord your God with all your heart and with all your soul and with all your strength."[59] Otherwise we would have never known. We will now live in a state of exquisite contentment, this state is described as shalom by the Jews, generally translated 'peace'. However, the word as generally understood by users of English only implies a lack of hostilities; shalom embraces a much wider concept than that; it includes wholeness, completeness, tranquillity, peace in the accepted sense, contentment, harmony, prosperity, satisfaction, and welfare. Shalom is synonymous with the Greek eiréné used close to 100 times in scripture. The term, in either language, conveys something that is only truly understood by the penitent regenerate with a broken and contrite heart. This is the peace that is beyond understanding; "And the peace of God, which transcends all understanding, will guard your hearts and your minds in Christ Jesus."[60] Renewed strength and power is found within the walls of the closet which has now become a stronghold, as David said, "You are my strength, I watch for you; you, God, are my fortress."[61]

It is in these secret places in which we are, paradoxically, totally vulnerable and absolutely secure, "Who can hide in secret places so that I cannot see them?" declares the Lord. "Do not I fill heaven and earth?" declares the Lord."[62] We are, by the Holy Spirit totally exposed, and by the same Spirit enclosed within a fortress. Let us reflect on the agonies of Jeremiah as he shares with us the reality of the possession of the broken and contrite heart, the truth of the poverty of the poor in spirit, "If you do not listen, I will weep in secret because of your pride; my eyes will weep bitterly, overflowing with tears, because the Lord's flock will be taken captive."[63] It is a symptom of agapé which obliges this soul to stand in the gap and intercede for a nation under judgement. He had been obedient to the Word of God and warned Israel of impending doom. Such a person will have had his soul purged of all impediments to him being in a state of divine union with his creator. His pleading was to no avail, but he had been obedient, and despite his various prophesies being totally fulfilled he kept his promise and wept bitterly in his secret places as we know from his Lamentations. Also to be learned from Jeremiah, is the depth of the calling to which one may well be summoned and the consequent cost which will have to be paid. However, it is these same secret places that "I will give you hidden treasures, riches stored in secret places, so that you may know that I am the Lord, the God of Israel, who summons you by name."[64] As we have discovered from the testimony of King David "One thing I ask from the Lord, this only do I seek: that I may dwell in the house of the Lord all the days of my life, to gaze on the beauty of the Lord and to seek him in his temple. For in the day of trouble he will keep me safe in his dwelling; he will hide me in the shelter of his sacred tent and set me high upon a rock."[65] He had found the stronghold in which all the treasures he could ever desire were to be found and they were his for the asking, in fact he did not even have to ask, they were part of his inheritance.

'Secret' is used advisedly in these contexts on account of two considerations; firstly because it is communicated and infused into the soul totally through agapé and the Holy Spirit, and is without the understanding and intellect, and so the divine knowledge is acquired without the testimony of any witnesses. Likewise, the enlightened cannot explicitly communicate these experiences to another soul because there are no means by which such exquisite spiritual revelations and pinnacles of comprehension can be properly shared. Many of those who have read the testimonies of the likes of King David, Job and Paul will remain largely unmoved since they cannot identify with them in any significant way. They are merely dead words because the reader is too rich in spirit and distracted to the extent that he or she will deduce, wrongly, that there is no message contained within the testimony which is relevant to themselves. They are the vain and arrogant who assume themselves to be sufficiently 'righteous' already by virtue of their works. Works of the flesh or the soul will not do, they are filthy rags in the sight of God. Someone will quote from James in a misguided attempt to gain justification by works. "Someone will say, "You have faith and I have works." Show me your faith apart from your works, and I will show you my faith by my works."[66] It has to be noted that the discussion in this passage is concerning faith. It has been established, hopefully, that faith is a state of koinonia with God and, in fact, is not evidenced by anything that one does, but by faith itself. James is addressing a generic congregation he describes as 'the twelve tribes scattered among the nations'. James, being a spiritual man, is countering the claim of some Jews that they are justified under the law and saying, in so many words, that it is *spiritual* fruit-bearers that are now justified and that they do not have to work at being fruit-bearers, it comes supernaturally! Jesus said, "*At my Father's direction* I have done many good works. For which one are you going to stone me?"[67]

"Blessed are those whose strength is in you, whose hearts are set on pilgrimage. As they pass through the Valley of Baka, they make it a place of springs; the autumn rains also cover it with pools. They go from strength to strength, till each appears before God in Zion."[68] The Valley of Baka also known as the Valley of Weeping. Those who have set out and endured the pilgrimage will have gone, by various means and tribulations from strength to strength. As with those who had literally gone through the Valley of Baka and were on the approach to their destination, which was Jerusalem; they find that in the very fact of their traverse they had made it a place of springs, and autumn rains had also covered it with pools. "His anger is but for a moment, His favour is for a lifetime; Weeping may last for the night, but a shout of joy comes in the morning."[69] As has been declared so often, the journey up the mountain and into the darkness of night have been wrought with contrast and divergence, with anguish and euphoria, with confusion and clarity, with blinding darkness and blinding light, with agapé and a sense of abandonment, with shalom and despair and frustration. Such are the ways of our enigmatic and resourceful God. Perhaps it is time for the pilgrim to give vent to the passions which have been aroused in his, now broken, heart and his, now impoverished, spirit with great shouts of joy, praise, and thanksgiving. Those who have wept, probably for much longer than a night, will find His favour so refreshing that they will have no thought or remembrance of those 'angry' moments. As Paul says "One thing I do: Forgetting what is behind and straining toward what is ahead."[70]

The lot of any person on a spiritual path is that they will never be aware of how far they still have to go because they will have no way of accurately assessing where they actually are. They will be aware that the alpha is somewhere behind, and that the omega is somewhere 'out there' but will have no perceptions of the time and distances involved in realisation of their goal, or even of what, precisely, their goal actually is. This is where many a pilgrim goes astray, this is where presumption leads to vanity, arrogance, self-righteousness, and blasphemy. Presumption is of the flesh, the understanding, and the intellect; faith is of koinonia with God, they are incompatible, they become a shaft of darkness, an intrusion into the light. Those who are proceeding in faith will realise that they are now having to come to terms with an entirely new paradigm.

They are assimilating the mind of Christ; they are starting to think as the apostle Paul was when he made this statement of his own state of mind. They are starting to comprehend the deepest thoughts that he was expressing when he made statements such as "My conscience is clear, but that does not make me innocent"; "Rejoice always and pray without ceasing"; "Pray in the spirit, not with words but with cries and groans"; "I serve the Lord with great humility and tears"; "I wrote to you with anguish and tears"; "I know nothing good dwells in me"; "Sorrowful, yet always rejoicing; poor, yet making many rich; having nothing, and yet possessing everything."; "Godly sorrow brings repentance that leads to salvation and leaves no regret, but worldly sorrow brings death."

As with the man who still did things he did not want to do, and still travelled widely having a thorn in his flesh which was distressing whether it had been physical or ethereal. The pilgrim will, because until these bodies are done with, still have to contend with the fact that he now has to live in a state of paradoxes. His refreshed, enlightened, and stimulated spirit will have to co-exist with, but not be dominated by, his soul. Thereby he will experience such phenomena as euphoric despair, an awareness of having everything but possessing nothing, of being victorious through surrender, of simultaneous stark darkness and blinding light, sense of abandonment and koinonia, total fulfilment and total frustration, a great treasure of no value, a desire for activity but no taste for it. He will be inebriated by agapé, fervently protect his gift of shalom (after all this is an invaluable indicator of our being in the centre of God's will) and will have lost all desire or need for recognition, status, or prestige. He will aspire to nothing having gained everything, have the richest of relationships having severed all blood and soul ties, he will have a sense of bewilderment from his excursions up the mountain and through the dark night and at once be totally orientated. He will be tormented by his own thorns but maintain his state of exquisite contentment. Everything will be totally comprehended by him to his own satisfaction and will remain beyond his own understanding, he will no longer need to know and consequently be told everything that he needs to. Thus, will be the evidence of his spiritual transitions and his successful integration with them. To quote a very wise man "Blessed is the one who perseveres under trial because, having stood the test, that person will receive the crown of life that the Lord has promised to those who love him."[71] This pilgrim will be souled out!

INDEX OF REFERENCES

Chapter 4

Chapter 5

Chapter 6

15 2 Kings: 23/25-26
16 Micah: 5/13-15
17 Micah: 7/9
18 Isaiah: 9/19
19 Isaiah: 10/5-6
20 Ezekiel: 7/5-9
21 2 Kings: 24/1-5
22 Luke: 1/50
23 Luke: 12/5
24 Luke: 2/5
25 John: 3/36
26 Acts: 5/3-5
27 Ephesians: 5/6
28 1 Thessalonians: 2/15-16
29 Revelation: 14/10
30 Revelation: 15/1
31 Revelation: 15/4
32 Revelation: 19/15
33 1 John: 4/16
34 Luke: 10/18
35 Matthew: 12/31

Chapter 7

1   Romans: 5/20
2   Luke: 10/25-28
3   Genesis: 2/17
4   John: 14/6
5   Genesis: 3/22
6   Revelation: 2/7
7   Revelation: 2/7
8   Deuteronomy: 32/35
9   Genesis: 3/16
10 Genesis: 6/4
11 Genesis: 6/6
12 Genesis: 6/5
13 Genesis: 6/7
14 Genesis: 6/8
15 Exodus: 33/19

Chapter 10

10   1 Kings: 11/38
11   Nehemiah: 1/9
12   John: 15/14-15
13   1 John: 4/16
14   Luke: 13/3-4

Chapter 11

1   Exodus: 3/15-16
2   Exodus: 4/5
3   Matthew: 22/32
4   Genesis: 31/13
5   Genesis: 32/3-5
6   Genesis: 32/6
7   Genesis: 32/7-8
8   Genesis: 32/9-10
9   Genesis: 32/11
10   Genesis: 32/22-23
11   Genesis: 32/10
12   Genesis 32/24
13   Psalm: 51/17
14   1 Corinthians: 4/4
15   Matthew: 7/21
16   Genesis: 32/25
17   Genesis: 32/26
18   Genesis: 32/27-30
19   John: 5/19
20   1 Corinthians: 2/16
21   Luke: 6/46
22   Matthew: 10/34-35
23   Luke: 12/51
24   2 Timothy: 4/3
25   Luke: 2/14
26   Acts: 16/30-31
27   Matthew: 7/21
28   Hebrews: 13/8
29   Galatians: 4/9-11

Chapter 12

1   Luke: 14/33
2   Luke: 14/27
3   Matthew: 22/14
4   Luke: 14/33
5   Matthew: 7/21
6   1 Corinthians: 3/11-14
7   2 Corinthians: 3/6
8   Romans: 8/29
9   1 John: 2/6
10 Matthew: 7/21
11 James: 5/19-20
12 Romans: 14/23
13 Romans: 16/25-27
14 Romans: 10/17
15 Isaiah: 64/6
16 Romans: 10/1-3
17 Matthew: 6/33
18 Ephesians: 2/10
19 Colossians: 1/9-10
20 Matthew: 5/16
21 1 Peter: 2/12
22 1 Corinthians: 3/15
23 Galatians: 5/16
24 Luke: 24/49
25   Acts: 2/1-4
26 John: 3/8
27 1 Corinthians: 2/9-10
28 Matthew: 11/25
29 James: 3/17
30 Psalm: 46/10
31 Isaiah: 40/31
32 1 Samuel: 15/22
33 Matthew: 7/16
34 1 Corinthians: 3/3-4
35 Acts: 17/11
36 Matthew: 7/22-23

Chapter 13

Chapter 14

25 Habakkuk: 2/3
26 Isaiah: 42/8
27 1 Corinthians: 1/25
28 Habakkuk: 3/19
29 Luke: 12/48
30 Matthew: 25/29

Chapter 15

1   1 Peter: 2/2
2   1 Corinthians: 3/2
3   Exodus: 33/19
4   Romans: 9/15
5   Ephesians: 3/19
6   1 Corinthians: 13/1
7   Genesis: 1/27
8   Isaiah: 40/13
9   Phillipians: 2/12
10 Psalm: 51/7
11 Matthew: 5/6
12 Psalm: 63/1
13 Luke: 14/28
14 Luke: 14/27
15 Luke: 10/27
16 Leviticus: 26/3-4
17 John: 15/10
18 Matthew: 7/21
19 Phillipians: 2/12

Chapter 16

1   James: 1/2-4
2   Thessalonians: 5/18
3   Ephesians: 1/11
4   1 Corinthians: 2/15
5   Psalm: 139/23
6   Luke: 18/11
7   Matthew: 20/25-26
8   Hebrews: 13/17

9   Matthew: 20/27-28
10 Luke: 22/25-26
11 Ephesians: 5/21
12 1 Peter 2/9
13 Matthew: 7/19-21
14 Acts: 6/3-4
15 Romans: 14/12
16 1 Peter: 5/3
17 Colossians: 2/8-9
18 Matthew: 7 /3
19 Matthew: 23/3-7
20 James: 5/20
21 Jeremiah: 5/21
22 Mark: 8/18
23 Luke: 19/26
24 Romans: 8/1
25 Ephesians: 1/11
26 Romans: 8/28
27 Romans: 7/15
28 Psalm: 139/25
29 James: 1/5-8
30 Matthew: 23/8
31 John15/1-10
32 James: 3/13-17
33 1 Corinthians: 2/16
34 John: 5/19
35 Jude: 1/25
36 Romans: 16/27
37 Philippians: 3/13-14
38 Philippians: 2/3
39 Matthew: 7/6
40 James: 4/3-6

Chapter 17

1   Colossians: 1/15-17
2   Luke: 14/26-31
3   Luke: 14/33
4   1 John: 2/6

Chapter 18

Chapter 19

Chapter 20

27 Job: 7/20
28 Psalm: 39/11
29 Job: 23/7
30 Romans: 8/17
31 2 Corinthians: 1/3-4
32 Acts: 14/21-22
33 Romans: 5/3-4
34 Job: 19/21
35 1 Peter: 2/21

Chapter 21

1   Psalm: 139/7
2   Deuteronomy: 32 /12
3   Jonah: 2/3-4
4   Jonah: 2/6-7
5   Psalm: 88/18
6   Ezekiel: 24/11
7   Job: 28/12
8   Job: 28/28
9   Proverbs: 2/7
10 Proverbs: 4/7
11 2 Chronicles: 1/10
12 1 Corinthians: 12/8
13 James: 3/14-15
14 Isaiah: 40/28
15 Jonah: 4/2
16 Romans: 9/16-18
17 Romans: 1/22-24
18 Romans: 9/19-20
19 Lamentations: 3/32-33
20 James: 1/2-3
21 Romans: 5/3-4
22 Job: 12/22
23 Psalm: 139/2
24 Psalm: 142/3
25 2 Corinthians: 10/5
26 Luke: 11/23
27 Psalm: 139/8-10

28 Habakkuk: 3/18-19
29 Psalm: 27/7-9
30 Romans: 11/33
31 Psalm: 8/3-4
32 Job: 12/22
33 Job: 13/3
34 Job: 42/5-6
35 Daniel: 2/22
36 Romans: 11/33
37 Luke: 8/10
38 Ephesians: 3/2-5
39 1 Corinthians: 2/9-10
40 John: 6/63
41 Matthew: 11/15
42 Isaiah: 40/31
43 Matthew: 6/6
44 1 Corinthians: 2/16
45 1 Corinthians: 3/1
46 Isaiah: 26/17
47 2 Corinthians: 3/3
48 Luke: 3/16
49 Matthew: 3/11
50 Deuteronomy: 4/24
51 Isaiah: 4/4
52 Hebrews: 12/28-29
53 Philippians: 3/10
54 Hebrews: 11/6
55 John: 5/19
56 Romans: 101/7
57 1 Thessalonians: 5/17
58 Colossians: 3/17
59 Deuteronomy: 6/5
60 Philippians: 4/7
61 Psalm: 59/9
62 Jeremiah: 23/24
63 Jeremiah: 13/17
64 Isaiah: 45/3
65 Psalm: 27/4-5
66 James: 2/18

Milton Keynes UK
Ingram Content Group UK Ltd.
UKHW010623121023
430452UK00001B/48

9 781803 814421